MW00848982

OCCUPY
— YOUR —
DESTINY

THE WINNING
STRATEGY FOR LIFE

GARY KEESEE

Occupy Your Destiny: The Winning Strategy for Life

Copyright © 2023 by Gary Keesee.

Unless otherwise noted, all Scripture quotations were taken from the New International Version® (NIV)® of the Holy Bible. Copyright © 1973, 1978, 1984, 2011 by Biblica, Inc.™ All rights reserved worldwide.

Scripture quotations marked (TPT) were taken from The Passion Translation® of the Holy Bible. Copyright © 2017, 2018, 2020 by Passion & Fire Ministries, Inc. Used by permission. All rights reserved. ThePassionTranslation.com

Scripture quotations marked (NLT) were taken from the New Living Translation of the Holy Bible. Copyright ©1996, 2004, 2015 by Tyndale House Foundation. Used by permission of Tyndale House Publishers, Carol Stream, Illinois 60188. All rights reserved.

Scripture quotations marked (NASB) were taken from the New American Standard Bible®. Copyright © 1960, 1971, 1977, 1995, 2020 by The Lockman Foundation. Used by permission. All rights reserved. Lockman.org

Scripture quotations marked (NET) were taken from the NET Bible®. Copyright © 1996, 2019 by Biblical Studies Press, L.L.C. Used by permission. All rights reserved. Netbible.com

Scripture quotations marked (AMP) were taken from the Amplified® Bible. Copyright © 2015 by The Lockman Foundation. Used by permission. lockman.org

Scripture quotations marked (BSB) were taken from the Berean Study Bible. Copyright © 2016, 2020 by Bible Hub. Used by permission. All rights reserved worldwide.

Scripture quotations marked (EHV) were taken from the Evangelical Heritage Version® of the Holy Bible. Copyright © 2019 Wartburg Project, Inc. All rights reserved.

Scripture quotations marked (ESV) were taken from the English Standard Version® of the Holy Bible. Copyright © 2001 by Crossway, a publishing ministry of Good News Publishers. All rights reserved.

Scripture quotations marked (NKJV) were taken from the New King James Version® of the Holy Bible. Copyright © 1982 by Thomas Nelson. Used by permission. All rights reserved.

Scripture quotations marked (KJV) were taken from the King James Version of the Holy Bible. Public domain.

Printed in the United States of America. All rights reserved under International Copyright Law. Contents and/or cover may not be reproduced in whole or in part in any form without the express written consent of the Publisher.

ISBN: 978-1-958486-49-8

Published by Free Indeed Publishing.
Distributed by Faith Life Now.

Faith Life Now
P.O. Box 779
New Albany, OH 43054
1-(888)-391-LIFE

You can reach Faith Life Now Ministries on the Internet at www.faithlifenow.com.

TABLE OF CONTENTS

INTRODUCTION

It's time to stop going through the motions.

Stop settling for anything less than the dream God gave you.

Stop talking yourself out of bold decisions.

Stop discounting your calling.

It's time to stop running from your vision... and to start occupying your destiny.

If you're tired of feeling like you're not living up to your true potential, you're not alone. We all have a sense that we were created for something more than just rising, working, and returning home to watch television, just to repeat it all again the next day. And when you finally regain your time on the weekend, you spend it catching up on home and life maintenance. While life has its demands and sometimes mundane tasks, surely there must be a greater purpose to our existence. And there is!

Gary's *Occupy Your Destiny: The Winning Strategy for Life* book offers winning strategies for creating an exciting and fulfilling life that makes you eager to face each day. Gary knows firsthand what it takes to succeed against all odds. Once a painfully shy young man, growing up intimidated to speak up or dream of success, Gary cried out to God for answers to his own destiny and how to break out of wishing for success to actually having it! Eventually, he became number one among 5,000 offices in financial services and saw his teachings on Kingdom principles and financial practices travel around the world.

Gary and I met as he was finishing his degree in Old Testament studies. He may have struggled to believe in himself, but he did believe in God and sincerely wanted to follow His plan. We married the following fall. Taking a position as an insurance salesperson was definitely a departure from his plans to pursue ministry, and totally out of character for his personality. He knew it was a divine direction for his life and development, but that didn't make commission sales less terrifying. Later, it would prove to be even more so than either of us could have dreamed.

The things he learned on his journey from shy, small-town boy, born prematurely and wearing correctional shoes, to becoming financially successful and having worldwide ministry impact are nothing short of a miraculous transformation.

In his down-to-earth, practical, and easily applied style, Gary will show you how to find your place and what it means to occupy until "He" (Jesus) comes. He explains biblical truths and direction with unique revelation that apply to everyday life. When we understand the times we live in, our unique place in the battle, and the tools we have to stand our ground, life gets exciting! Our work has new meaning, and we can see ourselves living far beyond the day-to-day grind.

We live in unprecedented times that suggest (actually scream!) we are racing toward the finish line. Every day, we see headlines that shock and perplex, compelling us to ask, "How can I do something important and make a difference, get off the treadmill, and live life for God's highest?

I know you want to have maximum impact and be rewarded for your days. Your life matters. You were placed here by your Designer for a specific purpose and destiny. Gary has lived it and continues to do so every day. I've witnessed the impact and the ripple effect of the principles he shares in this book. They work, and he is living proof! This is not an easy get-rich-quick scheme but a solid life of winning against all odds and occupying the space created just for you.

—Drenda Keesee

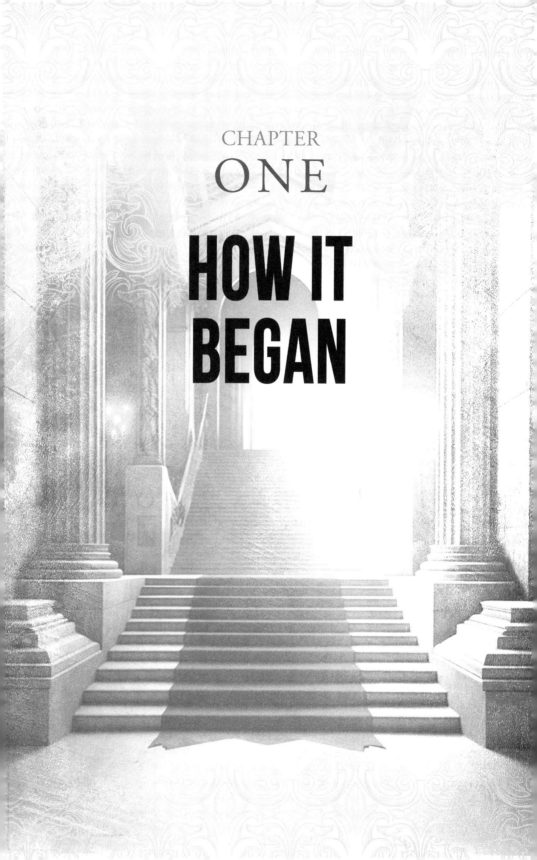

CHAPTER
ONE

HOW IT
BEGAN

The days were brutal! For nine years, Drenda and I lived in extreme debt and then, of course, extreme stress. Nine years! I wish it were only a brief detour along the path of life, but it was nine years. We lived in a world of survival, one day at a time. Money problems constantly raged through our minds. Bill collectors called us constantly, and fear tormented us with what seemed like endless hopelessness. During those years, I was in sales and lived on commissions. Although I really liked what I was doing, it never really paid the bills. We were always thinking that the next month would be better and we could get caught up, but that never happened. Instead, we slowly slid into debt. Ten maxed out credit cards, three personal loans with interest rates as high as 33%, two car payments, IRS liens, tens of thousands owed to relatives, and various other debts that we could not pay. One by one, we defaulted on all those accounts and found ourselves out of options. The shame during that season was palpable; maybe suffocating would better describe it. It sucked every bit of joy out of life. There were no options, no dreams, and no vision in that void. We had no idea how to get out of the quagmire that seemed to hold us hostage.

As Christians, we knew the Bible said that God was our answer and that He would provide for us, but we just could not seem to find that answer. Although we both loved God, were Spirit-filled believers, and attended a great church, we just did not know how to bring what we read in the Bible into reality in our lives. Well, as you can imagine, everything finally came to a head. There were no more debt options available. We had maxed out our credit cards and maxed out all our friends and family's generosity. No bank would extend any further credit to us, and our refrigerator was empty. We couldn't even pay the $300 a month rent for our little broken-down farmhouse.

The farmhouse was built in 1856, and no, it had never been remodeled. It still had the wavy glass in the windows, many cracked, which were held together with duct tape. It was carpeted with carpet that we found along the road in a trash pile. The mattresses in our kids' bedrooms were found in a nursing home's discard pile. The appliances were 30 years old, and there was no heat on the second floor. Mice, rats, bees, wasps, and hornets were constant companions. We would always be on the lookout for bees, wasps, and hornets. They would get into our clothes, and many times, we would hear the scream of one of our children when they put their arm in a coat or shirt only to be stung by a wasp or hornet. The cars were no better, and both had over 200,000 miles on them. So, when I say everything came to a head, I mean everything.

At this point in our discussion, let me give Drenda, my wife, huge credit. She is absolutely amazing! Although we lived in that little farmhouse, she made it into a home; and she gave me five of the most amazing children that I ever could have dreamt of. What was so amazing is that she loved me through all this mess and never gave up on me. For that, I am eternally grateful. I knew my family deserved better than what I was giving them, and I felt like such a failure. I had worked hard all of those nine years but just could not seem to break free from the financial hell I was living in.

On one particular day, the phone rang and the usual wave of panic came over me as I recognized the voice on the other end.

"Hello, Gary, this is so-and-so attorney. I have called you three times in the past about this delinquent account balance you have with my client, and all three times, you said you were mailing the check. This is my last call, Gary. If you do not have that check here by the end of three days, I will be forced to file charges against you on behalf of my client. Do you understand?"

"Yes," I mumbled.

Click.

I sat there stunned and full of fear. For some reason at that moment, even though I had been dealing with bill collectors for a few years, this time was different. I had no options. I knew it was over, I had nowhere to go, nowhere to hide. I set the phone down and slowly climbed the steps to my little bedroom and lay across the bed in tears, crying out to God for help. Very quickly, I heard the voice of the Lord. He simply quoted this Scripture:

> *"My God will supply all your needs according to His riches in glory in Christ Jesus."*
> —Philippians 4:19 (NASB)

I told the Lord that I knew that Scripture, but my needs were not being met! He answered my question immediately, "Yes, but you have never taken the time to learn how My Kingdom operates. In fact, most of My church lives as Israel lived in the Old Testament, enslaved to Pharoah, making bricks. They live a lifestyle of debt and live a lifestyle of financial bondage. I want My people free!"

I quickly ran downstairs, grabbed Drenda, and told her what the Lord had said to me. I repented to her for not seeking God and learning how His Kingdom works. We joined hands right there and asked God to help us understand what He meant. At that point, we really did not understand what He meant when He said I needed to learn how His Kingdom works. I began to study the Bible, and God began to speak to me and show me things that I had never heard before. Before I tell you what God taught me, let me say that understanding the Kingdom was like turning on a light in a dark room. For the first time, we found our answer!

GOD, WHAT DO YOU MEAN BY KINGDOM?

When God told me that I had never learned how His Kingdom works, I was confused, to say the least. Kingdom? Drenda had no idea what He was trying to tell us. So, we prayed, "Lord, teach us what You mean by Kingdom!"

The first thing I had to learn was what a kingdom was. I think this concept is hard for our western minds to grasp, living in an American mindset of democracy and free expression. God's Kingdom is not a democracy; it is a kingdom with a king. The authority of the king flows down through the kingdom through various government offices, which then bring the will of the king to the citizens of that kingdom. But let's understand that a mob of people by itself is not a kingdom. No, a kingdom is a mob of people that come under the authority and jurisdiction of a king's government and laws. Those laws lay out the king's will for his people. They provide the framework of life in the kingdom and lay out the benefits and duties of all the citizens of the kingdom.

> *Consequently, you are no longer foreigners and strangers, but fellow citizens with God's people and also members of his household.*
>
> —Ephesians 2:19

Stop everything! I finally saw it. The Kingdom of God is a government with laws. As a citizen living in that Kingdom and under the laws of that government, I had legal rights and benefits. The laws work for anyone and everyone in that Kingdom; they are not partial to any one person.

Laws do not change. We can send people to the moon because someone discovered the laws that govern the physical world. We fly in planes at 40,000 feet unafraid because we discovered the law of lift, which supersedes the law of gravity. We can put lights anywhere in the world that we want to because we understand the laws that govern electricity and lighting. Do you see it? Could it really be that simple? Laws! I then became a fervent spiritual scientist looking for clues.

I realized that my view of the Kingdom of God was all wrong. I had spent most of my life begging God to help me when all along I had the answer. When I was young, I was taught that no one knows what God will do; after all, He is God. When we prayed, we were taught that God answered prayer four ways: No, Yes, Wait, or Maybe. Wow, that really helped. But as I studied the Kingdom, I found out that God had already established what He gave us as citizens of His Kingdom—no begging required. It was all laid out in the laws of the Kingdom, and I had a legal right to all of it!

> *This is the confidence we have in approaching God: that if we ask anything according to his will, he hears us. And if we know that he hears us—whatever we ask—we know that we have what we asked of him.*
>
> —1 John 5:14-15

Take a close look at that Scripture and think about what it is saying. It is saying that if you ask anything according to the will of God, the laws of the Kingdom, you can be confident that God's answer is YES! This is not what most churches teach. They teach people that no one knows what God will do, that He is the one who brought the disaster, that He is the one who allowed that person to die of a hideous disease. But His will, expressed by the laws of His Kingdom, is clear. God heals! And He has given this legal right to every one of the citizens in His Kingdom.

HEALING IS THE CHILDREN'S BREAD

The King's law is clear: God heals. As an example, I was part of a big Christian rally a couple of days ago, and the evangelist was preaching about healing and encouraging the people to receive healing from God. Then, he told them how his wife died of cancer. His next sentence was, "But God is faithful." He went on to tell how he met a woman whose husband died of cancer, they were married, and how faithful God was in restoring their family. Now in most Christian circles, this is a perfectly normal story of how God works. However, it is not what the Bible says. Now, do not get me wrong. I am thrilled that God restored his family, but he missed something here. The Bible says:

> *__Is anyone among you sick__? Let them call the elders of the church to pray over them and anoint them with oil in the name of the Lord. And the prayer offered in faith will make the sick person well; __the Lord will raise them up__. If they have sinned, they will be forgiven.*
>
> —James 5:14-15

The evangelist said, "But God is faithful" in reference to his family being restored but not in regard to God keeping His Word regarding healing. How can God not fulfill His Word yet be faithful? He can't. He is always faithful! So, why are there apparent faith failures, situations where it appears that God is not faithful? We will discuss that, but first let me tell you a story that occurred after we had learned how God's Kingdom works and what our legal rights are in the Kingdom.

My daughter Amy, the oldest of my five children, had a huge tumor growing in her abdomen. The tumor had been growing for a couple of years and was causing her great difficulty. She had severe pain and digestive and urinary tract issues. She had just been married and did not want surgery as she may have lost the ability to have children; and her heart was always to have a large family. So, she did not pursue that option but instead spent time studying what God said about healing until she was totally convinced that healing was God's will for her. She then asked her mother and me to lay our hands on her for healing. Nothing happened at the moment we prayed, but two weeks later, she went to bed and woke completely healed. The pictures you see are eight hours apart! There has been no photoshop work done on them. She said she did not feel anything throughout the night, but she went to bed like the picture on the left and woke up like the picture on the right.

THE DIFFERENCE OF 8 HOURS!

BEFORE AND AFTER:
13 POUNDS AND 9 INCHES GONE!

She lost thirteen pounds and nine inches in her waist, and her back, which had been knotted and twisted, was completely rebuilt and was normal. She was healed.

BEFORE
Spine is straight,
intestines are
displaced, mass
in abdomen.

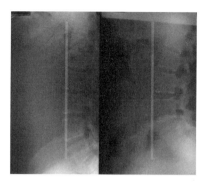

AFTER
Spine is curved,
intestines are
in place, mass
is gone.

My daughter-in-law had a tumor the size of a grapefruit in her abdomen and was told it was cancer and she had two months to live. Same thing: She was healed as she slept, with the tumor completely disappearing overnight. No chemo, no surgery, just the Word of God.

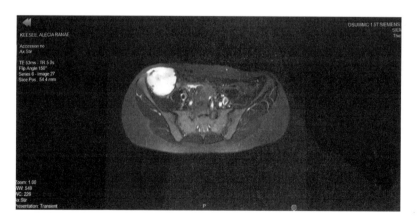

Do not get me wrong. I am not against doctors or anything that helps us get well, but rather, I am proving a point. The Bible does not change. God's laws do not change.

"So, Gary, why does it seem at times that God does not do what He says He will?" Great question, and I will give you a very brief answer here. My other books go into greater detail about this, but let's take a brief look at this question.

Let's look at a story out of the Bible.

> *When they came to the crowd, a man approached Jesus and knelt before him. "Lord, have mercy on my son," he said. "He has seizures and is suffering greatly. He often falls into the fire or into the water. I brought him to your disciples, but they could not heal him."*
>
> *"You unbelieving and perverse generation," Jesus replied, "how long shall I stay with you? How long shall I put up with you? Bring the boy here to me." Jesus rebuked the demon, and it came out of the boy, and he was healed at that moment.*
>
> *Then the disciples came to Jesus in private and asked, "Why couldn't we drive it out?"*
>
> *He replied, "Because you have so little faith. Truly I tell you, if you have faith as small as a mustard seed, you can say to this mountain, 'Move from here to there,' and it will move. Nothing will be impossible for you."*
>
> —Matthew 17:14-20

Okay, here is a story asking the same question that so many ask: "What went wrong?" I would like to point out that just a few chapters earlier, Jesus had already given His disciples authority to cast out demons. This is why they asked, "Why couldn't we cast it out?"

> *Jesus gathered his twelve disciples and imparted to them*

authority to cast out demons and to heal every sickness and every disease.

—Matthew 10:1 (TPT)

So, what was the reason the demon did not leave? Well, Jesus told us, *"You unbelieving and perverse generation."* Perverse is calling good bad and something bad good. So, in this case, assuming that God allowed the demon to stay in the boy and accepting that outcome when Jesus had clearly given them the authority to cast out demons would be considered perverse. The demon should have come out! Jesus clearly told them the reason the demon did not come out. He did not say it was God's will the demon stay there and torment that child. No, He proved that when He took over and kicked the demon out, and it left immediately. Jesus said unbelief was the reason, not that God changed His mind. They were not in faith, so heaven had no legal jurisdiction to make the demon leave. I know that what I have just said may seem strange to you.

So, let me ask you this: "Did Jesus ever face a situation that He could not fix?" Probably most people would answer that question with a no.

Take a look at Mark 6:1-2 and Mark 6:4-6.

Jesus left there and went to his hometown, accompanied by his disciples. When the Sabbath came, he began to teach in the synagogue, and many who heard him were amazed.

—Mark 6:1-2

Jesus said to them, "A prophet is not without honor except in his own town, among his relatives and in his own home."

__He could not do any miracles there__, except lay his hands on a few sick people and heal them. He was amazed __at their lack of faith__.

—Mark 6:4-6

That's right; Jesus could not heal them because they did not have faith. I think everyone would agree that Jesus had the ability to heal, but He did not have the jurisdiction to bring healing, the anointing of heaven, into that situation. He said they did not have faith. So, what is faith? Faith is simply being fully persuaded that what heaven says is true. (Again, trying to make a long story short here.)

FAITH IS SIMPLY BEING FULLY PERSUADED THAT WHAT HEAVEN SAYS IS TRUE.

"You made them a little lower than the angels; you crowned them with glory and honor and put everything under their feet."

In putting everything under them, God left nothing that is not subject to them. Yet at present we do not see everything subject to them.

—Hebrews 2:7-8

When Adam was placed on the earth, God gave him total legal jurisdiction over the earth. He was to rule over the earth on behalf of the Kingdom of God. The text implies that he was crowned with glory and honor. He probably did not wear an actual metal crown, but the analogy shows how Adam was to rule. He had the glory, the anointing of God, to rule, and he had the position to rule, the honor. Just like a government backs up a king's words, so would God back up Adam's words. But, of course, we all know that Adam lost his position of authority over Satan and actually rebelled against God's Kingdom.

So, let me ask a question here. When Adam had full authority over the earth realm, before he fell, how did Satan gain access to the earth? The text clearly says that there was nothing on the earth that was not subject to him, so we know that he had dominion over Satan. Satan could not come bursting in there to try and take over without going through Adam. Before he fell, Adam had full jurisdiction over Satan. Since Satan had no authority to take Adam's authority from him, he had to deceive Adam and Eve into willingly laying down that authority. What I am saying is, Adam was the legal entrance, the door, into the earth realm. Without going into a lot of detail, let's just get the understanding that Satan had to go through Adam to gain access in the earth realm. So, when Adam gave his authority to Satan, Satan then gained spiritual jurisdiction over him.

Then, the only way that God could regain access into the affairs of men was through the same door that Satan had to use, through a man. Although Satan had gained spiritual jurisdiction over mankind, men and woman still had the full lease on the earth itself, as it had been given to them. Just as Adam believed Satan and followed him, giving him that legal entrance he was looking for, God would have to find another man who would believe Him to give Him legal access again. That man's name was Abram. Abram believed God, and God made a covenant with him, which allowed God access through his life and lineage. Of course, Jesus came through that lineage, through that covenant.

Just as God was able to work through Abram, later to be named Abraham, through his absolute trust in God, the same is true today. Having that absolute confidence in what heaven says is called faith. Since Satan still has the legal claim over mankind that was given to him by Adam, heaven cannot move on the earth unless a man or woman is in faith, in agreement with what heaven says. So, in Mark 6, Jesus could not heal because there was no faith, no agreement between heaven and the earth realm.

I know this is a very short explanation, but it is vital that you understand this. This is why I have put an appendix on the topic of faith at the back of this book. This will help you understand more about how the Kingdom works, what faith is, and why faith is required before heaven can move. You will learn what faith is, why faith is required before heaven can move, how we get faith, and how to know if you are in faith.

YOU MUST KNOW THE LAWS THAT PERTAIN TO WHAT YOU WANT TO OCCUPY.

What I am trying to do in this first chapter is to provide a basic understanding regarding the laws of the Kingdom. This is because, as we are going to find out in this book, to occupy anything, you must know the laws that pertain to what you want to occupy. If you want to occupy a house, there are laws that you need to know in regard to purchasing, zoning, taxes, and more. So it is in the Kingdom of God.

You will need a basic understanding of Kingdom law and to have total confidence in those laws and the fact that those laws do not change. If circumstances seem to indicate that the laws of the Kingdom have failed, you will need to look for another reason, because the laws of the Kingdom cannot fail.

When they came to the crowd, a man approached Jesus and knelt before him. "Lord, have mercy on my son," he said. "He has seizures and is suffering greatly. He often falls into the fire or into the water. I brought him to your disciples, but they could not heal him."

"You unbelieving and perverse generation," Jesus replied, "how long shall I stay with you? How long shall I put up with you? Bring the boy here to me." Jesus rebuked the demon, and it came out of the boy, and he was healed from that moment.

Then the disciples came to Jesus in private and asked, "Why couldn't we drive it out?"

He replied, "Because you have so little faith. I tell you the truth, if you have faith as small as a mustard seed, you can say to this mountain, 'Move from here to there' and it will move. Nothing will be impossible for you."

—Matthew 17:14-21

Unfortunately, it seems that most Christians live like the father in our story with the demon possessed boy. "Jesus, please have mercy on me!" This is how most Christians pray; they beg. They then go into all the reasons why God should hear their case, trying to persuade God to move on their behalf.

"He has seizures and is suffering greatly. He often falls into the fire or into the water."

By explaining how the boy was suffering, the father was trying to play on God's empathy, trying to make a case that this was serious and deserved His attention. But this is all wrong! Asking for mercy implies that the one you are asking has the power to provide what you need but has not decided to help you. However, as you can see in this story in the Bible, that is not true. Once the correct understanding of the Kingdom and the will of God was restored in the situation through Jesus, the demon came out immediately. How fast? Immediately!

However, it seems that many, if not most, have judged the Word of God by what they have experienced rather than by knowing God cannot lie and thus immediately knowing there must be another explanation for the Word's apparent failure.

The majority of believers know that God has the power to kick out demons. So, they assume that since the demon did not come out that it is God's will that all demons do not come out. The result? We start a doctrine, or a denomination, that teaches that all demons do not come out. But there is a very simple reason the demon did not come out. Unbelief!

It is the jurisdiction issue!

Understanding spiritual jurisdiction answers so many questions as to why some things happen and why sometimes things do not happen. The reason the demon did not come out is it did not have to! There was no authority from heaven—faith—requiring it to leave the boy.

Wow! As Drenda and I began to learn these Kingdom laws and principles, our lives radically changed. We got out of debt in two and a half years and started multiple companies. Built and paid for our dream house on 55 acres of some of the prettiest land in Ohio. And the most amazing thing was that we were able to give hundreds of thousands of dollars to finance and support the Kingdom of God. I would often think, *Am I the same guy that was looking under sofa cushions to find enough change to buy a Happy Meal to split between three children?* Yes, I am. How all that happened and what God taught me is recorded in my Your

Financial Revolution book series. You can get them from Amazon or from my website, GaryKeesee.com.

Become a spiritual scientist! That is what I called myself after God began to teach me the laws of the Kingdom. I would read the Bible with a completely different mindset. I would look for clues as to how the Kingdom worked in each story. I knew that what I was seeing in each story or event in Jesus's ministry were Kingdom laws in operation, and I was desperate to learn them. "How did that happen?" or "Why did something not happen?" were the questions I asked. Every story is there to teach you. Hidden behind the shock and awe are Kingdom laws that are yours to use. As a citizen of the Kingdom, you can do the same things that Jesus did.

AS A CITIZEN OF THE KINGDOM, YOU CAN DO THE SAME THINGS THAT JESUS DID.

> *Very truly I tell you, whoever believes in me will do the works I have been doing, and they will do even greater things than these, because I am going to the Father.*

> —John 14:12

This book will hopefully uncover why so many Christians are not further ahead in life, not just financially but in influence, impact, and ministry. I hope that interests you, because this book is about you and a place called destiny, your destiny.

CHAPTER
TWO

WHERE ARE YOU GOING?

Let me start our discussion with what will probably sound like a very strange statement.

Christians spend most of their time at the Red Sea!

"What are you talking about?" you ask. Yes, the Red Sea. You remember when Moses split the Red Sea, and the nation of Israel walked on dry ground out of Egyptian bondage and into a new life, a new nation. Oh, what a glorious day that was! Can you imagine growing up only knowing slavery? In fact, as far back as you could remember, and as far back as your parents and grandparents could remember, it was the same—slavery. The dream of freedom must have been such a grand idea that I am sure they could not have even imagined what it would be like. Not only did Israel leave Egypt but also how they left was even more astonishing. Can you imagine seeing the plagues hit Egypt? Seeing the Red Sea split and the people walking out on dry ground? Then watching your enemy being blocked by a cloud of fire, giving you time to cross over to the other side, and then watching the water come rushing over that army—and knowing that you were then completely free to enjoy a new future? It must have been intoxicating! And then what about Exodus 12:35-36?

> *The Israelites did as Moses instructed and asked the Egyptians for articles of silver and gold and for clothing. The Lord had made the Egyptians favorably disposed toward the people, and they gave them what they asked for; so they plundered the Egyptians.*
>
> —Exodus 12:35-36

They were carrying gold and silver, as much as they could carry! What a day that must have been for those freed slaves, to actually be carrying gold and silver that was theirs! No wonder they sang and sang in worship after they crossed the Red Sea. But here is where we find a problem, a snare if you will, that even plagues God's people today and holds them back from reaching their future almost as much as slavery itself. "What possible snare could there be in such a great deliverance?" you ask. Making deliverance the goal and mistaking the beginning for the end. Let me explain.

When Drenda and I were in serious debt, I really could not see myself free financially. I used to think, *What would it feel like to not owe anyone money?* It was a dream so far from my perception of reality that I could not even see it. Debt was my enemy, the monster that I was believing God to conquer. As I said in the first chapter, everything around us was broken. Everything spoke of what we did not have. Everything spoke of failure.

When Drenda and I began to apply what God was teaching us about the Kingdom and He spoke to us concerning new ideas and new directions, we were so excited. I can remember the night He gave me a dream to launch a new business of our own, even though we had no idea how to do what He was showing us. But then to see that business begin to prosper in ways that we had never thought of, all I could say was, "Wow!"

I also remember around that same time that GM brought out their new Saturn vehicles. They were advertised to be small cars to compete with the Japanese cars that were flooding into the United States. Since I was in sales and I was on the road every day seeing clients, I wanted one of those new Saturns. Even though the new business was doing well, we were still climbing out of debt and did not have the extra money to pay cash for a new car, but God had a plan.

During the days of being severely in debt, I had leaned on my dad to help me get by. It was humbling, to say the least. My dad was not a Christian, and here we were, the Christians in the family, having to beg bread, so to speak, from him. It got to the point that when I called, he would say, "How much do you need this time?" Every time he said that, it stung me like a whip and emphasized the financial failure that I was. During those years in debt, I had borrowed somewhere just over $20,000 from my dad just to survive.

One day as my dad and I were walking and talking, he said, "I have made a decision. You do not have to pay me back. I will just make a notation that upon my death, the amount you owe me will be subtracted from your portion of the estate." I was shocked and elated and thanked him as this alleviated the awkwardness I always felt around him knowing that I owed him money.

One day, a check from an old insurance claim came. One that I had been expecting for over three years in the amount of about $22,000. I was so excited because this was the largest amount of cash I had ever had at one time, and it was more than enough to buy one of those new Saturn cars. The one I was looking at was $11,500, and I had made up my mind that I was going to buy one. As I was planning to go and purchase the new Saturn, the Lord spoke to me and said, "Do not take that money and buy your car. Instead, I want you to pay your dad back first."

I was shocked and acted like I did not hear that, but I could not get away from it. I knew I was supposed to go and pay my dad back. So, I called him to tell him I was heading over to see him. I did not tell him why I was coming over, but I took my checkbook as I was going to pay him back in full. I walked in, and he said the usual: "How much do you need this time?" I said, "Dad, I did not come here to get money, but I have come to pay you back in full." He sat there shocked. I could see tears slowly forming in his eyes, then he said, "Well, some of that money was a gift. If you write me a check for $10,000, we will call it even." Boy was that exciting! We hugged, and I thanked him, then in tears myself.

After Drenda and I left his house, we realized that we had about $13,000 left over, so we went straight to the car dealership and paid cash for that brand-new Saturn. Wow! When we paid cash for that car, what a feeling. After being in debt for nine years, just getting by, and then paying cash for a new car, we thought we had gone to heaven. But here is the point I want to make. The new car was amazing, and I loved it. But that car was not designed to just sit in the driveway now that I owned it debt free. No, that car was designed to go places; it had a job to do. You would think I was nuts if you came over to my house and the new car just sat in my driveway, and I had never yet driven it. You would think I had a problem. But this is what Christians do all the time.

I want to make a very important point here: Israel was delivered from Egypt to go somewhere. Slavery was just the obstacle holding them back from their destiny. That car was a tool to help me reach my destiny. Getting out of debt was not the end but the beginning. Debt was simply the roadblock that was holding me back from reaching my destiny. Do you see it? The church loves to talk and sing about deliverance. We spend a lot of time talking about casting out demons or singing about our new freedom in Christ.

ISRAEL WAS DELIVERED FROM EGYPT TO GO SOMEWHERE.

Do not misunderstand me. I worship God every day for the

authority He gave me over demons. I worship God every day for the freedom I now have in Christ. But just having authority over demons is not the final objective here. The demons are just obstacles trying to hold me back from my destiny. My freedom in Christ is not just so I can go to church and sing great songs of worship. No, my freedom in Christ is freeing me from the old mindsets and habits that were holding me back of course. But greater than that is my freedom in Christ, which has given me a new future full of purpose and destiny.

Remember this: Just as Israel was delivered from Egypt to go to a new land and start a brand-new nation, you, too, have a place that God has prepared for you to occupy for His Kingdom. You may not see it yet, but He has a plan, a place He is leading you to. He leads with only glimpses and dreams lest Satan get a full understanding of His plans for us and try to intercept them. But as we take one step at a time, one day at a time, always moving forward, God will reveal the entire picture to us as we mature.

> ...YOU, TOO, HAVE A PLACE THAT GOD HAS PREPARED FOR YOU TO OCCUPY FOR HIS KINGDOM.

This book is about getting you to a place called destiny—not just getting you there but showing you how to occupy that place once there.

Let me give you an example. Let's say you own a field. It is yours, it is paid off, and now it is under your legal jurisdiction. Now, let's say you never do anything with that field but just allow it to sit idle and grow weeds. Although you own the field and it is debt free, it is not being used. There is no tangible benefit from owning the field.

Even though you own the field free and clear, which in itself is a great victory, <u>you are not occupying the field</u>! You own it, but you are not occupying it; and you will never enjoy what you do not occupy.

So, now let's assume that you go a step further. You decide you are going to do something about those weeds. You go out and buy the best brush hog money can buy, and you mow down all the weeds on your property. With great satisfaction, you stand back and look at the field now clear of weeds. You also look at the great brush hog you have bought and think to yourself how you have really arrived to own such a piece of land and such a great brush hog. Yes, conquering that field, owning it, and even mowing down the weeds is a great accomplishment, but the objective of owning the field and cutting down the weeds has not yet been met!

The field was purchased to produce a harvest of grain and fruit. And, again, here is where the church stops. We go to our churches and sing and worship for the great things He has done for us. We celebrate our freedom in Christ and all the benefits of being a citizen of the Kingdom of God we are enjoying. We celebrate someone being set free from demonic addictions, someone now being debt free, someone being healed of cancer, all of which are great victories. Yet, the church loses sight of its ultimate purpose—to occupy a place called destiny.

I define destiny as a place that you are called to occupy and influence on behalf of the Kingdom of God. This does not necessarily mean ministry, although it could. God wants His influence to be expressed in every area of life. Think of destiny as a place of platform and influence. A dentist has a platform to influence others for Christ. That platform is the place of destiny for that dentist. It is where God will use him or her to be a light in a dark world.

Everyone has a place of influence where God has called them to be, to have a voice, to shine in the darkness.

> *They will be called oaks of righteousness, a planting of the Lord for the **display of his splendor**.*
>
> —Isaiah 6:13b

God is planting people in every occupation for the display of His splendor! So many are living so far below what God has for them because they just do not understand how or even that they should occupy the opportunities that God brings to them. I want to dig into this concept of occupying and help you understand exactly what this means for your life.

We're going to start in Luke chapter 19.

> *While they were listening to this, he went on to tell them a parable, because he was near Jerusalem and the people thought that the kingdom of God was going to appear at once. He said: "A man of noble birth went to a distant country to have himself appointed king and then to return. So he called ten of his servants and gave them ten minas. 'Put this money to work,' he said, 'until I come back.'"*
>
> —Luke 19:11-13

According to ebible.com, a mina was a Greek monetary unit worth 100 denarii, or about four months' wages for a normal citizen of the time.

The servants were not just to look at this money. They were to put it to work until he came back. The whole story is an analogy of Jesus Himself. He is going away, will be crowned King, and will come back as the King of kings and Lord of lords. The space between His going and then coming back as the King is the church age. That's you and me. He is giving some very important instructions to the church in this Scripture, and we need to pay close attention to it. I think the King James Version is how most of us learned this verse, so let's look at that.

> *He called his ten servants, and delivered them ten pounds, and said unto them, "Occupy until I come."*
> —Luke 19:13 (KJV)

"Occupy until I come."

So, who's He talking to? He is talking to you and me and giving a direct command concerning what we are to be doing while He is gone. But what does it mean? What is He commanding us to do?

In the dictionary, the word *occupy* means to take up a place or fill a space.[1] As you are sitting in your chair reading this book, I could say you are occupying your chair. You occupy it; you fill that space. The word could also mean to take hold of, or possess, or control a territory, or perform the functions of an office or position.[2] No one else can occupy your chair, because you already occupy it. You control it, and there is no room for someone else. If for some reason you get up from your chair, someone else could take it and sit in it even though your intention was to come right back.

Let me give you a really big clue to what I am saying: "Satan loves a vacuum." If you do not occupy it, control it, he will slide

1. https://www.merriam-webster.com/dictionary/occupy
2. Ibid.

into that seat and take control. Now, you can always kick him out again, but if you do not maintain occupation of that seat, someone else will sit there when all along God wants you in that seat.

Now, this is my opinion, and it is only my opinion, but one I think is valid. In my opinion, the church knows very little about occupying, very little about occupation. They have been taught some on deliverance but not much at all on how to occupy or what it actually means to occupy.

Most people cry out to God for deliverance, beg God for deliverance, remind God of the problems, and remind God of this and that, not realizing that they have already been delivered. They already have their answer.

> *For he has rescued us from the dominion of darkness and brought us into the kingdom of the Son he loves.*
> —Colossians 1:13

When you came into the Kingdom of God, when you called on the name of Jesus, at that point you were legally delivered or removed from Satan's jurisdiction. The King James Version of the Bible says the Father has "*translated us into the kingdom of his dear Son.*"

YOU ARE A CITIZEN OF GOD'S KINGDOM WITH LEGAL RIGHTS AND BENEFITS.

The word translated means to remove or change from one place to another.[3]

Let me say it again. You have already been delivered out of the jurisdiction of the enemy. No more begging. You are a citizen of God's Kingdom with legal rights and

3. https://www.merriam-webster.com/dictionary/translated

benefits. You are also a member of God's own household, so you have the inheritance as well, the entire estate.

As an example, let's say you were locked up in a prison cell where someone was holding you for a crime you committed. Then one day, the prison guard comes to you and says that someone has paid for your release. He then swings the door open wide and says, "You are free to go." But you just sit there upset because you are in jail. The door is open; you are free. Just get up and walk out. Satan has no more claim on you.

So many people ask me, "If I am already delivered, Gary, why am I having all this trouble?" That's a great question and one you need to find the answer to. Let me sum the answer up this way: If you don't know how to occupy the earth realm, Satan may be sitting in your chair!

SATAN MAY BE SITTING IN YOUR CHAIR!

Hang on. I have the rest of this book to help you understand what I mean and to show you how to take your place that God wants you to occupy for Him, so do not panic.

I pray that the eyes of your heart may be enlightened in order that you may know the hope to which he has called you, the riches of his glorious inheritance in his holy people, and his incomparably great power for us who believe. That power is the same as the mighty strength he exerted when he raised Christ from the dead and seated him at his right hand in the heavenly realms, far above all rule and authority, power and dominion, and every name that is invoked, not only in the present age but also in the one to come. And God placed all things under his feet and appointed him to be head over everything for the church, which is his body, the fullness of him who fills everything in every way.

—Ephesians 1:18-23

Paul says the reason he is praying this prayer for this young church is so they may know who they really are now that they have been delivered from Satan's grasp. The reason I took the time to write this book is the same—for you to know what you really have your hands on and who you really are in Christ.

*Know the hope to which he has called you, the riches of his glorious inheritance in his holy people, and his incomparably great power **for us who believe**.*

—Ephesians 1:18b-19a

I suggest you underline that phrase, "incomparably great power." There's no power that compares to it—NONE. And God says it is for you.

That power is the same as the mighty strength he exerted when he raised Christ from the dead and seated him at his right hand in the heavenly realms, far above all rule and authority, power and dominion, and every name that is invoked, not only in the present age but also in the one to come. And God placed all things under his feet and appointed him to be head over everything for the church, which is his body, the fullness of him who fills everything in every way.

—Ephesians 1:19b-23

Let me ask you an important question: If He's the head, who are the feet? That is an easy question, because Paul himself answers it when he says the church is His body. So, we—the church—are the feet of Jesus in the earth realm. And if that is so, then we can read this same Scripture from a personal perspective: Now we see that we also have been raised up with Christ far above all rule and authority, power and dominion, and that God has placed all things under our feet.

I know, I know what you are thinking: *That can't really be who I am.* Well, let's move over to the second chapter of Ephesians where Paul makes this even more clear.

> *And God raised us up with Christ and **seated us with him** in the heavenly realms in Christ Jesus, in order that in the coming ages he might show the incomparable riches of his grace, expressed in his kindness to us in Christ Jesus.*
> —Ephesians 2:6-7

Okay, let's just stop and take a deep breath. You have been seated with Christ, in the heavenly realms, on the right side of the Father. The right side of the throne is a seat of authority. Paul says that Jesus was seated far above all rule and authority, power and dominion, and every name that can be invoked. So, if we are seated with Him, then we also have been seated far above all rule and authority, power and dominion, and He has placed all things under our feet.

Now, let's allow that to change the picture of who we are. We are not just weak nobodies here on the earth. No, we are royalty. And catch this:

By the Spirit, we have the same authority Jesus has!

No, Gary, that cannot be true. We cannot have the same authority that Jesus has. Listen up. Paul says that we are seated with Christ, in the same place He is seated, on the right side of the Father. You are called to rule and reign with Christ and with His authority.

YOU ARE CALLED TO RULE AND REIGN WITH CHRIST AND WITH HIS AUTHORITY.

It started out as a normal church service, but it did not stay "normal" very long. Instead, it was a service I would never forget. Our church was young, probably only a year old, when this event happened. We were meeting at a Christian radio station that was allowing us to use their meeting rooms for our Sunday services. We had roughly about 70 to 90 people attending our services at that time.

This particular Sunday started out like any other, with a great time of praise and worship where God's presence was so tangible and awesome. I would usually come up to the platform toward the end of praise and worship and minister as the Holy Spirit led me. This time as I was on the platform encouraging and ministering to the church, I noticed a young woman sitting on the front row beginning to act in a peculiar way. I had seen this woman in church a couple of times before, and I knew that she was new to the church, a friend of some members who brought her. As I continued to encourage the people, amazingly, this young woman began to become more and more agitated. Then to my horror, she began to raise her dress over her head and slipped down to the floor. Again, this was directly in front of me on the front row. Although at the time I did not have much experience with demons, I knew enough to realize that I was dealing with a demonic personality that was tormenting this young lady.

I quickly walked down from the platform and began to rebuke the demon. The demon reacted with a show, as the woman actually levitated off of the ground. Drenda and I and two of my elders began to deal with this thing. I began to speak to this demon, stating that it had to leave. I was again amazed as the woman spoke with a man's voice and said, "This bitch is mine!" I corrected the demon, forbidding it to speak anymore, and we cast it out. If I remember correctly, we cast about seven different spirits out of the woman. When we were finished, she went completely limp, and a great peace came over her. We led her in a prayer of salvation and gave her some instruction as we knew the demons would try to come back after she left the church service. This young woman stayed in the church for a while before moving out of state. Today, she is happily married with a family, completely set free by the power of God.

Now, let me ask you: Did I have to beg God to help this young woman? Did I have to scream and yell to somehow convince God to move? No! I calmly exercised the authority that God had given me in this situation, knowing that the demon had no legal ground to stand on. And I had complete and absolute jurisdiction over it.

OUR LEGAL RIGHT TO ENJOY THE PROMISES OF GOD IS A LEGAL WORK; IT IS FINISHED.

Pay attention to our posture in Christ. Ephesians says we are seated with Christ. We are not running around frantically trying to do things in our own strength. No, our jurisdiction over Satan is a finished work. Our legal right to enjoy the promises of God is a legal work; it is finished. Yet as I said earlier, most people's prayer lives are ones of begging and hoping.

To help you understand how life is supposed to work, let's look at a police officer directing traffic. The police officer is a normal human being, yet he is able to stop a multiton truck with one word. Why? The truck could just run over the man if the driver wanted to. But it stops, not because of the man but because of the badge. The driver knows that the entire government of the state, and ultimately the United States, is there to enforce the words of the officer.

That is EXACTLY your position in Christ and how you are to operate. A king rules with a command, and his government carries it out or backs it up. The same is true for us spiritually. We have been given the authority to rule and reign in life.

> *Truly I tell you, whatever **you** bind on earth will be bound in heaven, and whatever **you** loose on earth will be loosed in heaven.*
> —Matthew 18:18

> *"Have faith in God," Jesus answered. "Truly I tell you, if anyone says to this mountain, 'Go, throw yourself into the sea,' and does not doubt in their heart but believes that what they say will happen, **it will be done for them**."*
> —Mark 11:22-23

Done for them? By whom?

> *Are not all angels ministering spirits sent to serve those who will inherit salvation?*
> —Hebrews 1:14

You are here on the earth ruling on behalf of the Kingdom of God, and heaven backs up your words.

So again, let me make it clear that when you came to Christ, you were delivered from Satan's grasp! And, of course, as people come to Christ, we do have to deal with some strategies and some strongholds in our lives to which the enemy may be trying to hold us hostage. There is a ministry of deliverance. But again, it is not the end; it is the beginning. And I need to remind you that if you are dealing with the enemy, you are not "trying to defeat him." He has already been defeated. You are simply operating from a place of authority over him with the authority Jesus has given you.

Even though deliverance is so needed and awesome, we need to always understand that deliverance is step number one on our journey to destiny. You see, when you're delivered, you're delivered from somewhere or something to go somewhere. You need to have a picture of that, and I think the church doesn't talk about that much. Of course, we hear and sing about going to heaven one day, but when Jesus gave the disciples the command to occupy, they were on the earth, and that is where they were to occupy. If we talk about deliverance, and we need to, we also need to understand that we have a purpose beyond deliverance, beyond that freedom—a place that God has designed for us to occupy on behalf of His Kingdom.

> WE HAVE A PURPOSE BEYOND DELIVERANCE, BEYOND THAT FREEDOM—A PLACE THAT GOD HAS DESIGNED FOR US TO OCCUPY ON BEHALF OF HIS KINGDOM.

Now, we need to talk again about this term occupy. What does this really mean? What was Jesus really saying when He told us to occupy until He comes? What does it take to occupy something? I think if I asked, a lot of people would answer that question with the answer "power." I could agree it does take power to conquer something, but this is not what Jesus is implying when He said to occupy. Jesus told us to occupy the earth realm between the time that He was going away until He came back as a King. When He went away, it would have been after the resurrection; and Satan would already have been defeated. So, our command to occupy is not referring to conquering Satan. Yet today, so many Christians have this mindset that we are here to conquer Satan, and they pray for more power: "I need more power. I need more power." That's not true. We just read that you have already been given what? Incomparably great power.

> ...*that you may know the hope to which he has called you, the riches of his glorious inheritance in his holy people, <u>and his incomparably great power for us who believe</u>.*
> —Ephesians 1:18b-19a

You already have access to incomparably great power. There's no other power that is greater than the power that you have in Christ. Right? We do not need to pray for power; we already have it. We are the temples of the Holy Spirit, as well as having been baptized in that power by the Holy Spirit.

> *But you will receive power when the Holy Spirit comes on you; and you will be my witnesses in Jerusalem, and in all Judea and Samaria and to the ends of the earth.*
> —Acts 1:8

No, we have all the power there is. There is no more power than the power that we already have.

The reason we pray for power is because we don't understand authority.

You need to mark this down somewhere, or mark this page, because this is a statement you MUST understand to be able to occupy.

Going back to our police officer illustration, the truck doesn't stop because the police officer has the power to stop the truck. As a man, the truck has much more power than he does. No, the truck does not stop because the officer has more power but because he has authority to stop the truck.

To occupy has less to do with power and more to do with authority and administration.

CHAPTER
THREE

HOW DOES A KING RULE?

It is interesting to hear people pray. Have you ever heard someone praying, and they will say, "Jesus, Jesus, Jesus" over and over again? Or they say, "In the name of Jesus" 40 times in one prayer? I believe they pray like that because they have no confidence in the authority they stand in. They think if they say that name over and over again, their prayer will have a greater chance of being heard or will carry greater authority. In contrast, did you ever see Jesus praying, "Father, heal them"? No. He would simply say, "Be healed." That was all. He simply gave the command, and it was done.

Listen, you do not have to feel like you have authority to operate in authority. You do not need to feel His anointing to know you have authority. It is a legal issue, and He has given it to you. For instance, if I was yelling out to my kids in the backyard to come in, would I have to say, "Hey, kids, I am your dad, so come in the house for lunch"? No, that would be ridiculous. I would simply say, "Hey, kids, get in here; it is time for lunch." I would not have to prove I had the authority to tell them to come in. I know I have authority, and they know I have that authority. It is sad, but a large majority of the prayers that people pray are nothing more than unbelief with no authority.

> *And when you pray, do not keep on babbling like pagans,*
> *for they think they will be heard because of their many words.*
> *Do not be like them.*
>
> —Matthew 6:7-8a

One of the trademarks of Jesus's ministry was that He talked as one who had authority.

*The people were amazed at his teaching, because he taught them as one who had **authority**, not as the teachers of the law.*
—Mark 1:22

How do you talk? You should be talking like Jesus talked. I'm serious. Watch how He ministered, and do the same.

I remember when Jesus made this clear to me in a dream that I had in 2010. I was facing some difficult situations and kept praying and asking (I was really begging) God to help me. In the dream, I was on a horse. In my right hand I had a big sword, and I was on top of this big hill—by myself. But below me were hundreds of my enemy, all with swords as well. They were lined up facing me and were preparing to charge. I began to charge down the hill toward the entire army of enemy soldiers all by myself while crying out the word, "THOR!" Then the Lord said, "Don't underestimate yourself, Gary."

I awoke and immediately wanted to know what the word Thor meant. This was before the Avengers' movies, by the way. Now, everyone knows what Thor means. But then I had to ask some people who understood names and languages. They said Thor was the Son of Thunder. All of a sudden, I understood what the Lord was telling me. He was telling me that when the enemy sees and hears me coming, I sound like thunder. I have His authority!

At my 2010 Provision Conference, I was sharing my dream, and I was just telling the crowd what the Lord had spoken to me—that when the devil sees and hears me coming, it sounds like thunder. At that exact moment, a loud clap of real thunder filled the auditorium. It had not been raining, and in fact, it never did rain. This was the only clap of thunder heard all night. When I looked outside, the sky was clear except for one small cloud. I thought it was a great amen. I knew that God did that just for me and, of course, for those who were there.

The motto of the story was this, "Gary, you have My authority. Use it! Do not look at yourself as you see yourself in the natural. See yourself as I see you, and do what Jesus would have done in any situation you face." Wow! What a moment that was, and when you understand what God was saying to me, you can have some wow moments as well.

So, let's take a few moments and follow Jesus as He ministered and observe how He did it. Let's go to Matthew 9.

> *Jesus stepped into a boat, crossed over and came to his own town. Some men brought to him a paralyzed man, lying on a mat. When Jesus saw their faith, he said to the man, "Take heart, son; your sins are forgiven."*
>
> *At this, some of the teachers of the law said to themselves, "This fellow is blaspheming!"*
>
> *Knowing their thoughts, Jesus said, "Why do you entertain evil thoughts in your hearts? **Which is easier: to say**, 'Your sins are forgiven,' **or to say**, 'Get up and walk'? But I want you to know that the Son of Man has authority on earth to forgive sins." **So he said to the paralyzed man**, "Get up, take your mat and go home. Then the man got up and went home. When the crowd saw this, they were filled with awe; and they praised God, **who had given such authority to man**.*
>
> —Matthew 9:1-8

Please look closely at this Scripture. Notice how Jesus operated. He operated from a place of authority. "*Which is easier: to say, 'Your sins are forgiven' or to say, 'Get up and walk'?"* How did Jesus release His authority? With words! He said to the paralyzed man, *"Get up, take your mat and go home."* Then the man got up. Notice that <u>power follows authority</u> in this story.

Power follows the release of authority!

This is why I said people do not have a power issue; they have an authority issue. Also note that Jesus did not pray to His Father to heal this man. Please write this down somewhere: He did not pray to His Father to heal this man. Jesus already had the authority to heal this man. All He had to do was to speak!

My first experience with authority in the Kingdom happened when I was first baptized in the Holy Spirit. At the time, I knew nothing, really nothing, about the Kingdom of God. I did know a couple of Scriptures, but that was about it.

HE DID NOT PRAY TO HIS FATHER TO HEAL THIS MAN. JESUS ALREADY HAD THE AUTHORITY TO HEAL THIS MAN. ALL HE HAD TO DO WAS TO SPEAK!

I grew up in the pizza business since I was in junior high. Still to this day, my family has the same two pizza shops they have had for over 50 years, and they have done and are doing very well. Today, of course, I do not run them. My brother does. He has worked there since he was 12. But during that season in my life, I was tasked by my dad to run one of the shops, which I loved by the way.

I was a new believer, and having just been baptized in the Holy Spirit, I was so excited to tell anyone I could about Jesus. In those days, there was no Internet and no VCRs, so the young people would usually gather wherever they could to have a party. That place was my place. Our pizza shop was the only business open until 1:00 a.m. in our town, and the kids would fill the parking lot. It was an interesting place after 11:00 p.m. on a weekend night. There were always fights going on and people getting drunk. I usually had to go out and chase off a few of them to make room for our customers. At the time, I was only 18 myself. I knew most of them by name and tried to allow them some freedom to stay around.

But after I was baptized in the Holy Spirit, I had a different plan. I would invite anyone who wanted to stay around after we closed to stay for my little Bible study where I would read and discuss the Bible. Of course, I really did not know much about the Bible, but I was passionate about how my life was changing. I always offered free pizza, of course, and that is what really lured them in, not me with my Bible. On Friday nights, we always had many pizzas that were not picked up, so instead of throwing them away, I used them to lure the kids into the shop. I usually had 9 to 12 of the gang stay around to hear what I had to say and to eat pizza.

As I worked in the pizza shop, I would also share with my staff how my life had changed since I had become a Christian. Most of them were teenagers like me, and they were a captive audience.

Finally, one of them, Dave, asked me how to become a Christian.

That question had me stumped. I remembered that I had prayed to receive Jesus when I was in fifth grade, and I remembered praying at the little church with the revival, but I wanted to make sure I was on the right track since now people were looking to me for the answers. So, I looked in the Bible, and I found this Scripture.

And everyone who calls on the name of the Lord will be saved.

—Acts 2:21

Well, I thought, *that is how it is done.* So, I had him sit down in a chair, and I simply told him to say "Jesus." After I gave him my instruction, he just sat there. I was surprised. I repeated my instruction, "Dave, just say the name 'Jesus.'" Again, nothing. He just seemed to stare straight ahead, but I noticed that his body was quivering. Then, just as if someone uncorked a bottle, with great effort, he yelled out "Jesus!" And with that, great peace came over his face. I asked him what had happened, and he said he had heard me but that he could not speak. It was like something was holding him back. Then, with an effort, he was able to push through that feeling and say the name of Jesus. He told me as he said that name, a great peace came over him, and he knew he was born again, a Christian.

So, I thought that was how it was done. When anyone I was talking to wanted to become a Christian, I would sit them down in that chair and have them say the name of Jesus. And without exception, every single person had the same experience that Dave had. At first, they could not say that name, then with great effort, they would shout it out.

One of my favorite days at the shop was always dough making day. The mixer was in the back room, and at the time, I was the only person that made it. I usually made the dough after the evening's busy time, so maybe around 9:00 or so I would start. I always tried to make enough dough for three days, so I only had to spend time making the dough two or three times a week. I should also clarify that I would be making the dough for both restaurants. So, it took a couple of hours each time.

Well, this one evening, I was back in the back making the dough when there was a knock at the back door. As I opened the door, I recognized one of the young men, but the other one I had only seen come into the pizza shop a few times. The one that I had talked to before said that both he and his friend wanted to receive Jesus as their Savior. Well, I knew what to do. I sat the one I knew down in the chair and told him to say the name of Jesus. Just like Dave, at first, he could not say it and began to shake. Then, in a sudden outburst, he said the name, and there was peace.

I then planned to sit the other young man down in the chair, but I did not know where he went. As I looked around, I saw him up against the wall making motions as if he was trying to get away from something. I was puzzled. At this time in my life, I had never encountered a demon, and I knew very little about them. As the boy was struggling up against that wall, I was confused as to what was going on. Obviously, something was not right. So, I said, "Jesus, what is this?"

Instantly, it was as if a curtain was pulled open, and I saw a creature hanging on his side. The creature looked a little like a monkey, but its body seemed out of proportion. It was maybe three to four feet tall, if it were to stand up, but it was hard to say as its arms and legs were wrapped around the boy's body. Its face did, in fact, look somewhat like a monkey's, but it had a more pointed face. Its arms seemed longer than a monkey's and were very thin. Other than that, it was hairy like a monkey. The most prominent feature that caught my attention was its eyes. They were red, beady eyes, and they were staring straight at me. The look in those eyes can only be described by one word: hatred. Intense hatred. Hatred you could feel. I have never felt such an evil presence before.

As those eyes stared at me, my immediate response was to yell out loud. But then, I had a thought. The name of Jesus is how we are saved, so I decided to use that name in that moment. All I said was, "Jesus!" Instantly, the curtain closed. The demon did not leave, but I simply saw a fading image of it. If you remember the early television picture tubes, when you turned off the television, the picture slowly faded away and did not instantly disappear. At that moment, the boy bolted for the door and ran out. I was shaken by it all.

Two hours later, he came to the back door again, this time by himself, and was white as a ghost. He said, "The devil has been laughing at you ever since I left here. I have been hearing audible laughing for a while." I said, "No, the devil has not been laughing at me but at you! Please consider calling on the name of Jesus." But at those words, he bolted again and ran. I have not seen him again since that day, but I have heard from those that knew him that he eventually gave his heart to Jesus. Praise God.

Using the name of Jesus and seeing that demon respond to that name and my words had a lasting impact on me. I obviously never forgot it. It was a major clue as to how the Kingdom works, but of course back then, I did not pick up on that. I just knew that something happened when I said that name!

JESUS GAVE YOU HIS NAME AND HIS AUTHORITY TO USE.

Yes, there is authority in that name, and you need to understand and be confident in the fact that Jesus gave you His name and His authority to use. You will never be able to understand what Jesus meant when He said to occupy if you are not confident in that authority.

*After he put them all out, he took the child's father and mother and the disciples who were with him, and went in where the child was. He took her by the hand **and said to her**, "Talitha koum!" (which means "Little girl, **I say to you, get up**!"). Immediately the girl stood up and began to walk around (she was twelve years old). At this they were completely astonished.*

—Mark 5:40-42

Here we see the same formula. Jesus spoke, releasing His authority, then the power showed up and performed what He said. Again, Jesus did not pray to His Father; He spoke. An interesting note: Jesus was speaking to a dead body, not a dead girl!

*Jesus got up, rebuked the wind **and said to the waves**, "Quiet! Be still!" Then, the wind died down and it was completely calm.*

—Mark 4:39

Again, the same formula: authority first, then the power showed up. In this story, Jesus was talking to the waves and wind; and again, He did not pray to His Father for help. Pay close attention. He spoke to the waves! He said, "*Quiet! Be still!*" Then the wind died down and was completely calm. As I said, most believers are begging and crying out to God for deliverance, or help, or whatever, not realizing they have already been delivered from Satan's grasp and they now have the authority to deal with life. Are you getting this?

The next day as they were leaving Bethany, Jesus was hungry. Seeing in the distance a fig tree in leaf, he went to find out if it had any fruit. When he reached it, he found nothing but leaves, because it was not the season for figs. Then he said to the tree, "May no one ever eat fruit from you again." And his disciples heard him say it.

—Mark 11:12-14

In the morning, as they went along, they saw the fig tree withered from the roots. Peter remembered and said to Jesus, "Rabbi, look! The fig tree you cursed has withered!"

"Have faith in God," Jesus answered. "Truly I tell you, if anyone says to this mountain, 'Go, throw yourself into the sea,' and does not doubt in their heart but believes that what they say will happen, it will be done for them. Therefore I tell you, whatever you ask for in prayer, believe that you have received it, and it will be yours. And when you stand praying, if you hold anything against anyone, forgive them, so that your Father in heaven may forgive you your sins."

—Mark 11:20-25

Let's pay attention. "***He said to the tree***, *'May no one ever eat from you again.' And the disciples heard Him* **say it**."

Now at first, it sounds like He's being unfair to this tree. If you study the olive tree, the buds of the fruit come out at the same time the leaves come out. And they would actually eat those green olives before the season.

Now, let me ask you this: Here in Ohio, if I said, "When is apple season?" what would you say? The fall? Why? Because apples are ripe then. Are there apples in the trees before apple season? Yes. They're green, right? Have you ever eaten a green apple? Have you ever picked a green apple before the season, before they were ripe? Of course you have. I am not saying I like green apples, but Drenda loves them because they are tart.

This is exactly what is happening here in this story. When Jesus went to that tree, there should have been those small, green olives growing there. The leaves were there, but there was no fruit. So, He spoke to the tree. He cursed it. Again, let's be sure we see this. He spoke to a tree!

> *"In the morning, as they went along, they saw the fig tree withered from the roots. Peter remembered and said to Jesus, "Rabbi, look! The fig tree you cursed has withered!"*

Peter remembered. What did he remember? He remembered hearing Jesus speak to that tree. He said, "Rabbi, look. The fig tree you spoke to has withered." And Jesus said, "Have faith in God." Jesus was basically saying (my paraphrase), "Guys, look, this is how the Kingdom operates. You heard Me speak to this tree, and it responded to My words."

Jesus then went on to say, "I tell you, if anyone [does what?] says to this mountain..." That's an inanimate object! "...Go throw yourself into the sea and does not doubt in their heart, but believes that what they say will happen, it will be done for them."

THE AUTHORITY WE OPERATE WITH IS DELEGATED AUTHORITY AND IS NOT OF OURSELVES.

There's the power. Again, this is how the Kingdom works—releasing the authority of the Kingdom with the power following. You speak, and heaven backs it up. We need to remember that we can only speak what heaven says, however—what God's will is—in any situation. The authority we operate with is delegated authority and is not of ourselves.

I think so many see themselves from a before Christ perspective. But the Bible says you are a new creature in Christ Jesus; the new has come, and the old has passed away. We need to spend some time studying what the new is instead of dwelling on the old. I am telling you to study what Jesus says about you.

*Very truly I tell you, whoever believes in me will do the works I have been doing, and they will do even **greater things** than these, because I am going to the Father.*

—John 14:12

He is talking about you, the church, His body. But again, let's remember we do not need more power. We need to understand authority and how it flows down from the head. Jesus is never recorded praying to God to fix a problem. He said to the paralyzed man, "Get up, take your mat, and go home." He said to the dead little girl, "Get up." He said to Lazarus, "Come out." He said to the waves, "Quiet! Be still." He said to the tree, "Die. I curse you." But now it's your turn. What are you going to say?

Truly I tell you, if anyone says to this mountain, "Go, throw yourself into the sea," and does not doubt in their heart but believes that what they say will happen, it will be done for them.

—Mark 11:23

I remember when I was a student at Oral Roberts University, we had a required chapel service. In one of those services, a pastor named Fred Price came to speak. You may remember who he is.

At the time, I had never heard of him. He was teaching out of Mark 11:23 and pointing out how the authority of the Kingdom is released. Of course, coming out of a denominational church background, I had never heard anything like what he was saying. We were always taught that God did what He wanted to do, and that was it. But He was teaching like we had authority and heaven backed up what we said. I thought, *This man must be crazy!* I pulled my Bible out and was shocked to find he was indeed reading it word for word. *Oh, my goodness,* I thought. *It does say that.* Whatever I say!

Again, we can see the authority is released with our words, and then power backs them up. Satan does not want you to know this and is always going to try to deceive you out of your authority. This is why Paul was praying that this young church in Ephesus would get the revelation of their place in the Kingdom and how they, as believers, were raised up and seated with Christ in heavenly realms, having complete dominion over Satan and his demons.

AUTHORITY IS RELEASED WITH OUR WORDS, AND THEN POWER BACKS THEM UP.

So don't be so impressed with the devil or demons. You have absolute authority over them. Remember that deliverance is only providing freedom to advance toward your purpose and destiny. Demons work amidst a vacuum of authority. They are kind of like cockroaches. They like the darkness and will attempt to fill any space where there is not light. The only time you will see them is if you turn the lights on.

When we lived in Tulsa, we bought an old house. Drenda always did a great job of keeping it clean, but we were shocked when we would turn the lights on at night and see roaches scurrying across the floor back to the darkness. It was not until we put poison in the cracks and crevices and cleaned out every cabinet with any open food items that we finally cleared them out. To just come into our home in the daytime—it was perfect. This is exactly how the devil likes to operate. First, I had to learn how to use my authority to be delivered from those roaches. Then, I had to learn how to occupy that space so they could not come back. **Deliverance is <u>never permanent unless you learn how to occupy; they always try to come back.</u>**

Demons always try to come back!

Because of this, you need to know much more than deliverance. You need to know how to occupy your place of freedom and stay in your chair of authority that Jesus gave you to sit in.

I didn't know a thing about this growing up. I grew up, as I said, in a denominational church that did not teach me a thing, at least as I remember, about demons or my authority over them. When God called me to go to Bible school and then on to college, I began to learn some about demons and our authority as believers. Up until that time, the only experience I had with a demon was the time I saw the demon at the pizza shop. But there's book knowledge, and then there's actual knowledge, right? You learn knowledge from experience.

You may have already heard my story of how I woke up paralyzed one day and the spirit of fear attacked my life from my other books and material. But in case you have never heard it, I want to repeat it here—because it taught me a lot about what it means to occupy.

I woke up on a normal day and found that I could not feel my legs, arms, or face. They were all numb. My tongue was also numb. I was perfectly healthy the night before with no symptoms of any kind. As I woke, great fear came over me. I woke Drenda and told her what was going on. She immediately began to pray for me, and I began to pray also. Slowly, I found that I could move a bit, slowly got out of bed, and stood up. My heart was beating like crazy, and I felt horrible. The Bible says fear is torment, and I can attest to that. It was hell on earth.

Over the next couple of weeks, I dealt with severe panic attacks. One night, I could not stand it and called an ambulance to take me to the hospital. They did all kinds of tests then came back and said I was healthy and just having a panic attack, and they gave me some antidepressants. During those couple of weeks, I learned that my body would respond horribly to any kind of sugar I ate, with an almost instant panic attack. The antidepressants were not really helping too much. I did not know what was wrong with me, but it felt like I was dying. I was afraid to leave my house and afraid to eat anything with carbs in it.

Our income came from me meeting with clients in the evenings at their homes, and this was not happening. So, you can probably guess where our finances were. They had gone down to almost nothing. It was not like we were making a lot of money when I was healthy, but then nothing was coming in.

I knew that God healed, and I cried out many times for Him to heal me. But looking back on that, I was not in faith. I was simply desperate and begging. I did not know how the Kingdom worked at that time. I knew that God had the power, but I knew nothing about authority. The Bible says:

> *You believe that there is one God. Good! Even the demons believe that and shudder.*
>
> —James 2:19

They know He has power. And if you ask anyone, even an unbeliever, if God has the power to do things, they would answer, "Oh yeah, of course." But what Satan doesn't want you to find out is that you have authority. God's power backs up His authority.

So, I was just crying out, "God, heal me," but nothing was changing. A few weeks went by, and I was in torment. I couldn't sleep, I had heart palpitations, and I dreaded the night as I would have horrible thoughts all night long. As long as I stayed busy during the day, I could keep my mind occupied. But at night when things settled down was the worst time. I knew that God was my answer, yet I had no idea how to bring the Word of God into reality.

> **WHAT SATAN DOESN'T WANT YOU TO FIND OUT IS THAT YOU HAVE AUTHORITY. GOD'S POWER BACKS UP HIS AUTHORITY.**

On a Wednesday night service, I went to church, and this thing hit me the minute I walked into the church. At the time, I did not know what the issue was. Doctors had all kinds of names for things that were wrong with me. I remember one doctor saying that my hormones were all messed up and I would most likely become a diabetic. He said that it would be an interesting case to watch progress. What? I could not believe my ears: an interesting case to watch progress? I did not want to progress. I was living in torment then; I did not want it to get worse. Doctors were giving me different opinions. Hypoglycemia was one they were sure I had, which meant my blood sugar was all over the place. Although they had various names for things they thought were wrong with me, I was about to find out that it was a demon that was messing with me.

In the middle of the pastor's message, I was desperate enough to get up and go to the front of the church for some help. Now, you know what would happen in most churches if you did that, right? The security staff went on full alert and began coming toward me to head me off from reaching the front. But one of my good friends was also on staff there, and he was up on the platform that night sitting on the side. He jumped up and told the pastor, "It's okay. I know this guy. He's safe." The pastor slowly walked over to the edge of the platform and looked down toward me. He did not come down and lay hands on me. He looked at me for a second and then said, "Oh, he's got a spirit of infirmity." He then rebuked the spirit in the name of Jesus. He spoke to the spirit.

And man, the power of God hit me. I was knocked to the ground and was surprised to hear myself yell out with a loud groan at the same time. Instantly, I felt normal. If you're sick and if you have been sick for a while, it feels great to feel normal. I'm telling you, sickness is horrible. It's horrible. I hate it. I was so excited when I got up from the floor. I was free. I mean, I felt great.

So, we went out to eat at Pizza Hut after the service. I felt great! We sat down to order, and they had some music playing there. I do not remember what was playing, but I remember something about it bothered me. As I was sitting there, something just seemed to be all wrong. The music started agitating me, and then all of a sudden, that yucky, horrible feeling came back over me. I was confused, because I thought that God had healed me.

DON'T BUY THE LIE! STAND ON THE PROMISE OF GOD.

So many people lose their healing, lose the promise they've stepped out into because the enemy taunts them, and they say, "Oh, I thought that God had healed me, but I guess He hasn't because I now have symptoms again." Don't buy the lie! Stand on the promise of God. You need to keep that helmet of salvation on, the thoughts of God! The enemy is trying to bluff you!

The panic attacks and fear came back as they were before, but I was encouraged. The fact that it left was my first clue that it was a spirit, because it reacted and obeyed my pastor. I kept studying the Word of God, and the Holy Spirit kept showing me things. I was getting stronger but still fighting that horrible, sick feeling, panic attacks, and tormenting thoughts.

A few more weeks went by. Then one day as I was in my office and feeling really horrible, suddenly, I heard God speak to me up out of my spirit: "You need to speak to that spirit and tell it to go. And when you do, pay no attention to your emotions or how you feel." During those days, I had been saying, "I still feel bad. I'm not healed yet. I still have pain, so I'm not healed yet." I kept examining all the symptoms in the physical realm and agreeing with them that I was not yet healed. But that morning, God spoke with a stern voice and said, "Stop that! You take authority over that spirit and tell it to go."

Now, I was in a corporate office setting and had a couple of my employees around me. So, I decided to get up and rebuke that spirit in a more private place. I went to the restroom, and although I didn't know much, I knew what God had said, "Pay no attention to your emotions, but speak to that spirit and tell it to go."

I didn't have any fancy words. I just said, "In the name of Jesus, I bind you, you spirit of fear. I tell you to leave now in the name of Jesus." "Father, I thank you that I am free. Thank you that I am free." I felt no change at all, but I remembered what God had said: "Don't pay attention to your emotions or how you feel." So,

I thanked Him again. "Thank you, Father, that I am free. Thank you I am free." Although I felt no change, I went back to my desk and continued to thank the Lord that I was free. Twenty minutes went by. Every time I thought of how horrible I felt, I would again thank God that I was free. After those twenty minutes, I began to shake under the power of the Holy Spirit, and I saw that demon leave. A black, wispy form just left my body and went right up through the ceiling.

I was so thrilled; I felt completely normal. I was happy because then I knew how to deal with that thing. I knew it was a demon, and I knew how to take authority over it. I immediately called Drenda and told her it was gone and what had happened. We decided to celebrate with some Chinese food for lunch. Well, it tried to come back. The demons will always try to come back. But I knew how to handle them when they tried. Then, I knew. Not my pastor, not my spouse, but I knew that I have authority over demonic spirits and I had no need to be afraid.

YOU MUST KNOW HOW TO STAY FREE, CARRY OUT YOUR ASSIGNMENT, AND OCCUPY THE TERRITORY GOD HAS INSTRUCTED YOU TO TAKE.

Again, deliverance by itself is not enough. You must know how to stay free, carry out your assignment, and occupy the territory God has instructed you to take. The enemy is very persistent, like a dog chasing you down the street. And like a dog, the best thing to do is to stop, turn around, and face it. As you know, once you turn and face the dog, it usually backs off. But the demon will check to see if the door that was once open is still open and will try to come back.

I remember the first time it came back, I said, "Oh no, you

don't. No, not doing that. Nope. In Jesus's name, you're out of here." And it would leave immediately. For the first week, it tried to come back at least once a day, then once or twice a week, then once or twice a month. But I was not concerned; I understood my position of authority.

People are praying and begging God for something they already have.

You can't operate in authority if you're begging God for it.

You must know who you are, where you're seated, and what authority you have. Does that make sense? The Bible says, "Whatever you bind on earth, heaven backs up. Whatever you loose on earth, heaven backs up." Heaven is waiting on you, friend. Heaven can't do anything until you operate in the authority that heaven has given you.

Heaven doesn't have jurisdiction here unless you bring it here. So, that's why we need to understand what's going on here. This is life and death stuff. You need to understand this. I am taking so much time talking about authority because you will never be able to occupy anything unless you totally understand the authority you have been given and where you are seated in Christ. Let me give you a couple more examples.

My family on my dad's side has a hereditary issue with fatty tumors. It is a tumor that is usually just under the skin. It's a benign tumor, but it's a hindrance. My dad and siblings all had a lot of them, but I never had one. About three months ago, I had a fatty tumor show up on the back of my neck. I was not too concerned about it, but the fatty tumors cause lumps under your skin, which I did not like. So, I began to look at some information that would tell me how to get rid of them. I was shocked to find out there was no cure for them. According to what I read, surgery is the only way to get rid of them.

Well, I was not too fond of that answer, so I decided to use my faith to get rid of it. I told my kids, "Come over here." I said, "Put your hand there. You see that big lump there? That's a fatty tumor. I'm cursing it, and I want you to watch what happens to it. I want you to watch this." I would just lay my hand on it once a day, and I cursed it and commanded it to shrink and to disappear. Sure enough, it gradually began to go down in size until 30 days later, it was completely gone. There is now no evidence of it ever existing. I had another tumor show up under my fingernail. My fingernail began to get all warped, and as I researched what to do about it, I found the same thing: There's no cure for it. I told Drenda, "I'm cursing this thing," and I cursed it. Interesting, as my fingernail grew out, there was a distinct line between the warped portion of the fingernail and the new nail. The new nail was completely perfect as it was growing out. Deuteronomy 28:27 says tumors are a curse. I'm not putting up with curses, and neither should you.

The bottom line is this: The church needs to understand its authority. It's not power we need; we already have that. It is an understanding of the authority Jesus gave us. We have been given that authority not just to be delivered from Satan's grasp but to occupy territory here in the earth realm on behalf of the Kingdom of God.

CHAPTER FOUR

DELEGATED AUTHORITY

As we have been studying the authority we have in Christ, my prayer is now you realize that you HAVE the authority. When you have authority, you act and speak like it. This is so important to our topic of occupying that I cannot emphasis it enough. If I was giving you a quiz right now and asked you how we release heaven's authority into the earth realm, what would you say? If you said with words, you would be correct. And if I asked you how heaven's power is released into the earth realm, what would you say? If your answer was through authority, I would give you an A for the day.

> *Then Jesus came to them [this is after the resurrection] and said, "All authority in heaven and on earth has been given to me. Therefore go and make disciples of all nations, baptizing them in the name of the Father and of the Son and of the Holy Spirit, and teaching them to obey everything I have commanded you. And surely, I am with you always, to the very end of the age."*
> —Matthew 28:18-20

Let me paraphrase this. He said, "All authority in heaven and on earth has been given to me. Therefore, go...." I would like to make the point that until the resurrection, Jesus did not have all authority in heaven and on the earth. It was only after He defeated Satan that He could say, "and on the earth." But since this was after the resurrection and He had all authority on earth, He told His disciples to go, carry that authority with them, and declare His victory over Satan. He did not say to go and conquer; that part was finished. They were going out to administer justice, to proclaim and apply the laws of the Kingdom of God to the citizens of the earth realm.

There is a great Scripture in Isaiah that brings us a clear picture of what had just taken place.

The people walking in darkness have seen a great light; on those living in the land of deep darkness a light has dawned. You have enlarged the nation and increased their joy. They rejoice before you as people rejoice at the harvest, as warriors rejoice when dividing the plunder. For as in the day of Midian's defeat, you have shattered the yoke that burdens them, the bar across their shoulders, the rod of their oppressor. Every warrior's boot used in battle and every garment rolled in blood will be destined for burning, will be fuel for the fire.

For to us a child is born, to us a son is given, and the government will be on his shoulders. And he will be called Wonderful Counselor, Mighty God, Everlasting Father, Prince of Peace. Of the greatness of his government and peace there will be no end.

—Isaiah 9:2-7a

"For as in the day of Midian's defeat…." The battle is over. Battle garments are no longer needed. It is time to divide up the plunder. The devil has been defeated! Let me say it again, "The devil has been defeated!" We are not on a conquering mission any longer. We are on a mission to occupy. Now, Jesus is sending us out with His authority and His legal victory. We are to tell the citizens of this world who have not heard that they can walk free that the price for their freedom has been paid and Satan can no longer hold them hostage!

WE ARE NOT ON A CONQUERING MISSION ANY LONGER. WE ARE ON A MISSION TO OCCUPY.

And I tell you that you are Peter, and on this rock I will build my church, <u>and the gates of Hades will not overcome it</u>.
—Matthew 16:18

The King James Version says, "*and the gates of hell shall not prevail against it.*"

The gates are down. Gates are defensive, and they have been torn down. Satan's kingdom is now open for plunder. Jesus says it this way in the book of Mark.

"These signs will accompany those who believe: In my name they will drive out demons; they will speak in new languages; they will pick up snakes with their hands, and whatever poison they drink will not harm them; they will place their hands on the sick and they will be well."
—Mark 16:17-18 (NET)

Or again, how can anyone enter a strong man's house and carry off his possessions unless he first ties up the strong man? Then he can plunder his house.
—Matthew 12:29

Jesus is the one that tied up the strong man. <u>We can plunder his house!</u>

The day was a beautiful day in Maui, as most days are. Drenda and I were just taking some time off and enjoying the island. We love to rent a jeep and drive around, go to beaches, and hike up mountain trails. This particular day was windy, and we wanted to go up to Ho'okipa Beach Park to watch the wind surfers there. The park has been famous for wind surfing since the 1930s, and we always enjoy stopping by if the wind is up. This day was perfect, and the crowded parking lot verified that fact. We finally did find a spot to park.

As we were sitting and watching the dozens of surfers out on the water, I suddenly heard a blood-curdling scream: "My baby!" I could tell that this was a scream of desperation and shock. The scream was not far from me. In fact, it seemed only a few cars away. I jumped out of the car and began to run toward a woman who was holding a baby in her arms and crying hysterically. The baby was motionless. What I found out was the woman had come to watch the surfers. Since the baby was asleep, she walked down to the ocean for a better view, leaving the baby locked in the car. It was a very hot day, and the sun was intense. When the woman came back to the car, the baby was unresponsive. I could see the baby was red from the heat and was indeed unresponsive and not breathing.

I knew the situation was dire. I also knew that I had authority to deal with this if the woman would grant me jurisdiction to do so. So, I asked her if I could pray for the baby, and she said yes. I laid my hands on

> WE WERE ABLE TO SHARE WITH THOSE AROUND US THE NAME OF JESUS AND THE AUTHORITY THAT WE OPERATE IN. IT WAS A SIGN TO THOSE THERE THAT THERE IS AN ANSWER FOR LIFE'S PROBLEMS, AND IT IS JESUS.

that baby and commanded life into that child and for the child to wake up. Instantly, the baby's eyes began to flutter, and then she began to cry. The baby would be fine. The mother was so happy and relieved. We were able to share with those around us the name of Jesus and the authority that we operate in. It was a sign to those there that there is an answer for life's problems, and it is Jesus.

As I have said already, Jesus has given us absolute authority over the devil. But now, in this chapter, I want to go deeper into this topic of authority and show you Satan's greatest weapon against the church.

Do you remember the story I shared about the police officer in chapter two? That although he was just a man, he could stop a multiton semitruck just by holding up his hand and saying stop. I said that the truck then stops not because the driver is afraid of the man but of the badge. The truck could easily run over the police officer, but the truck driver stops because of the badge. He knows the government has the power to enforce the officer's every word with dire consequences for the truck driver if he doesn't stop.

To understand how a kingdom operates, we need to realize that a kingdom has a king who holds absolute authority over the kingdom. That authority is dispersed throughout the kingdom through many different positions. These positions hold a limited amount of authority as they relate to the position they are occupying for the king. The people in these positions do not have all authority, only the authority needed for their positions and to accomplish their assignments. All of these people are operating under what is called delegated authority, which is how any government or corporation works. Picture a company's organizational chart. There could be a few people, or there could be thousands, all working with limited authority in various assignments under the king or president of the corporation.

> THE PEOPLE IN THESE POSITIONS DO NOT HAVE ALL AUTHORITY, ONLY THE AUTHORITY NEEDED FOR THEIR POSITIONS AND TO ACCOMPLISH THEIR ASSIGNMENTS.

For instance, in May of last year, our government in this nation had about 24 million employees, counting state, local, and federal employees. Now, what are their jobs? Their jobs are to make sure that the will of the government, the laws, are assimilated into the population, to ensure that they are being upheld, and the citizens have all the benefits that are legally theirs. They also make sure that the citizens are safe and any evildoers are dealt with. So, if we think of the government, we think of millions of positions across the entire country. Of those 24 million positions in our federal, state, and local governments, those positions are all different. People are holding different responsibilities; different talents are needed in different places. But each one of those millions of employees have authority only in the place and assignment that has been delegated to them. If the government gave you a position, they would also give you the authority to occupy and fulfill that place of responsibility—but again, only in the area you had been given responsibility over. I don't have authority over your home. I don't have authority over your kids. But you have authority over your home and your kids.

Now, let's go back to that police officer. I think we all can agree that he had authority, but what if he went to a different city without being moved there by his boss? He just got tired of standing on the same street corner day after day and wanted to see something different. Even though he had a badge, knew the laws, and had skills as a police officer, if he went to a different city without being assigned there, would he have authority there? No! You see, the officer operates under delegated authority. He has no authority of his own, only his delegated authority. That authority is limited and defined.

I have staff at my church that sometimes I will send out to buy something for me, and I will give them my credit card to do so. In other words, I have delegated my authority to them to use for a specific area and assignment. They are operating under delegated authority. But if they went out and decided to buy a house and a few new cars with my money, that would be illegal, and they would be put in jail for that. Even though they are on my staff and had my credit card, that would not give them absolute authority to use any amount of funds they wanted and to purchase anything they wanted for themselves.

Here is a very critical part of the ability to occupy. In a government, there are thousands of different jobs needed. Down the line from the king, who has the absolute authority, are thousands of positions where people are operating under delegated authority. They represent the king all the way down to every citizen in the kingdom. Managing this flow of authority requires a great amount of administration.

Authority cannot flow down through a broken or disjointed system of administration.

In such a case with everyone out of place, there is no authority represented with power. And this is where the body of Christ seems to be stuck.

See, most Christians view their walk with God as it's me and God. And it is you and God with respect to your salvation and your heart, but it is not you and God in reference to function and your assigned position in the government of God. Now, do not misunderstand what I am saying. Every believer has absolute authority over the devil and demons. You are a Christian. You're going to heaven. Your salvation is secure in Christ. But as far as your position in this government, it's not up to you. Jesus is the head of this government, and He knows where you need to be. He told me, "My people do not understand delegated authority, and this is why the church is weak." That police officer does not have authority everyplace he walks. He only has authority that has been delegated to him by those who have authority over him, and usually, it is confined to a very specific location or assignment.

If Satan can disrupt the flow of God's authority by getting people out of their delegated positions, there will be no authority and only chaos.

I want to remind you that occupation is more about authority and administration than power. It is not about conquering. When I talk about authority in regard to occupation, I am usually talking about administering delegated authority. To help you get a picture of what occupation means, I want to reference some historical facts.

During World War II, on August 15th, 1945, Japan surrendered to the Supreme Commander of the Allied Powers, US General Douglas MacArthur. The first item on his agenda was to remove the weapons from the Japanese army. At the time of their surrender, their army numbered about seven million people. They were able to remove or demilitarize 88% of that army in three months, then destroy the weapons. And then the second item on his agenda was to reform Japan's constitution, or basically rebrand, relaunch, and redesign the nation of Japan. Because as you know, they had emperor worship, and the whole structure was not conducive to freedom.[4]

So, they designed a new constitution, building much of it

---

4. https://history.army.mil/books/wwii/macarthur%20reports/macar thur%20v1%20sup/ch5.htm

around the US Constitution. On November 3rd, 1946, they put this new constitution in place. It took thousands of men and women to help Japan accomplish this transformation and help rebuild the nation that had been shattered by war.[5] The occupation lasted from the end of the war in 1945 until 1952. During that occupation, nearly one million Allied servicemen served in Japan.[6]

My question to you is this: What were they doing while they were there? They were not fighting the Japanese. They were not there with a mindset of conquering the Japanese. Why? They'd already surrendered. So, what were they doing? They were rebuilding the nation under their new government, their new constitution, changing its structure, changing how their government worked.

That's our job as well. See, Jesus already conquered, and now we are here to change dysfunction to function, sickness to health, poverty to prosperity. Under our new government that Jesus brought into the earth realm, we are bringing this Good News of the Kingdom to the citizens of the earth realm. We are not conquering Satan's kingdom; that has been done. We are administrating the Kingdom's laws.

Administer means to provide or apply: dispense, and that is what we are called to do.[7]

Let me give you another example from Hebrews 11.

5. https://www.history.com/this-day-in-history/new-japanese-constitution-goes-into-effect
6. https://en.wikipedia.org/wiki/Occupation_of_Japan#:~:text=The%20occupation%2C%20led%20by%20the,nearly%201%20million%20Allied%20soldiers
7. https://www.merriam-webster.com/collegiate/administer

And what more shall I say? For time will fail me if I tell of Gideon, Barak, Samson, Jephthah, of David and Samuel and the prophets. Through faith they conquered kingdoms, <u>administered justice</u>, gained what was promised.

—Hebrews 11:32-33a

In this very concise and amazing statement, the writer of Hebrews gives us a very simple understanding of how to obtain the promises of God.

1. **Conquer** - Jesus did that for us.

2. **Administrate justice** - This is our responsibility. We are the police officers in the earth realm, so to speak. We are to administer the laws of the Kingdom, and heaven backs them up.

3. And step into the promise - or **occupy the promise**.

Let me explain what this tells us. Let me go back to my field illustration that I mentioned a while back. Let's assume I bought a field, and it was full of weeds. (1) The first step needed to make the land valuable to me would be to conquer the weeds. So, I mow them all down. Great, but there is still no benefit to owning the land yet, no profit. (2) So now, I must administer justice. Justice means the administration of law,[8] and the law specifies what is right. Unless I plant something on that land, unless I administrate what should be planted there, no profit will be produced. This is how it works. Once you put in place what should be there, (3) you capture the promise, or the original intent or benefit from the land.

---

8. https://www.merriam-webster.com/collegiate/justice

This is what the church is called to do now. We are to administrate justice, God's justice, His laws, and occupy the earth realm on His behalf. And how is that done? Through delegated authority and every person doing their part, in their assigned position.

WE ARE TO ADMINISTRATE JUSTICE, GOD'S JUSTICE, HIS LAWS, AND OCCUPY THE EARTH REALM ON HIS BEHALF.

Satan's most successful strategy to hinder the church is for people not to understand delegated authority.

Now, we may understand authority, but we need to understand delegated authority if we're going to be effective. To look at that, we're going to look at a very famous story of the centurion in Matthew 8.

> When he entered Capernaum, a centurion came to him asking for help: "Lord, my servant is lying at home paralyzed, in terrible anguish."
>
> Jesus said to him, "I will come and heal him."
>
> But the centurion replied, "Lord, I am not worthy to have you come under my roof! Instead, just say the word and my servant will be healed. For I too am a man under authority, with soldiers under me. I say to this one, 'Go!' and he goes, and to another 'Come!' and he comes, and to my slave 'Do this!' and he does it."
>
> When Jesus heard this he was amazed and said to those who followed him, "I tell you the truth, I have not found such faith in anyone in Israel! I tell you, many will come from the east and west to share the banquet with Abraham, Isaac, and

Jacob in the kingdom of heaven, but the sons of the kingdom will be thrown out into the outer darkness, where there will be weeping and gnashing of teeth."

Then Jesus said to the centurion, "Go; just as you believed, it will be done for you." And the servant was healed at that hour.
—Matthew 8:5-13 (NET)

Jesus was so impressed because this guy got it. He understood being under authority, being in authority, and that authority is released by what someone in authority says.

"Just say the word and my servant will be healed."
"I say to this one, 'Go!' and he goes, and to another 'Come!' and he comes, and to my slave 'Do this!' and he does it."

Now, this centurion was a commander of 100 men in the Roman army. The head of that army was Caesar. So, here is how authority flows down the chain of command. When the centurion takes an order from his commanding officer, it should sound exactly like Caesar's voice to him, just as if Caesar himself gave the order. And when he gives a command to his men, it also should sound exactly like Caesar's voice to his men. What would happen if that centurion decided that he did not agree with what Caesar's voice sounded like one day, did not like the orders and just changed them slightly? What if down the entire chain of command, they all did that? Do you think the Roman army would have a chance of winning many wars? Not a chance! It would be nothing but defeat and chaos.

This is exactly what Satan's plan for the church is—defeat and chaos. He wants to get everyone out of order so that the authority from the King is perverted and does not flow down through the government, leaving a mess behind.

What if this centurion decided to go over to another regiment and tried to order them around? I mean, he is a centurion, right? He has the uniform and credentials. But one problem, he has no authority over that other regiment.

This is not being taught in the churches. People criticize leaders without thinking about it. They go to a church and then leave a church without really thinking about staying submitted. Everyone is out of order: No one knows who to listen to or submit to. This is why the church is weak and we do not see the power of God there. Remember, power follows authority. The fact is you cannot have authority unless you are submitted to authority. But today, authority is a bad word.

> *Submit yourselves, then, to God. Resist the devil, and he will flee from you.*
> —James 4:7

You have no authority unless you are submitted to authority. You may ask this question: "How do you submit to God?" Well, if the commander we mentioned above wanted to submit to Caesar, how would he do that? Would he try to reach out to Caesar personally and ask him what he should be doing? Of course not. He would submit to his commanding officer, not to Caesar directly, unless of course he was assigned to report directly to Caesar himself.

How does a church member submit to God? Of course, the church member must submit to God in his heart, but he also must submit to those who have authority over him. So, when James says to submit to God, it also means to submit to those God has put over you. I doubt this goes over well with our "if I don't like it, I leave it culture." So let me say it in a clearer way. If you cannot be corrected without getting offended or quitting, you are not ready for promotion. Why? Because you are not submitted to authority. Here is a major key for you to remember.

Who are you to submit to, and who is to be submitted to you?

When Paul was teaching Pastor Timothy how to pick leaders for his church in Ephesus, he gave Timothy some advice.

> *He must manage his own family well and see that his children obey him, and he must do so in a manner worthy of full respect. (If anyone does not know how to manage his own family, how can he take care of God's church?)*
>
> —1 Timothy 3:4-5

It was not enough that his children simply obey him. They should also do it with full respect. Full respect of what? The father's authority in the home. Paul implies that if they do not understand this most important law of delegated authority, they would have no idea how to manage the church. Why? Because the whole church is held together by delegated authority.

Satan's greatest plot against the church is division. He knows if he can cause division in the church, then the authority used against his kingdom will fail. Why? Because a house divided against itself will not stand.

This principle does not just apply to the church but to business as well.

Every kingdom divided against itself will be ruined and every city or household divided against itself will not stand.
—Matthew 12:26b

If you are trying to operate outside of your delegated authority (meaning trying to exercise authority outside of your legal area of jurisdiction), essentially, you are tearing God's Kingdom down, and you will not stand. Let me ask this again: "Where has God called you to be?" I did not ask, "Where do you want to be?" I asked, "Where has God called you to be?" God will test each of us and train us to submit to authority before He will put us in authority.

GOD WILL MAKE A WAY FOR YOU WHEN HE FINDS YOU FAITHFUL. STAYING SUBMITTED AND LOYAL WILL PAY OFF IN BIG DIVIDENDS IN YOUR LIFE.

So many people today have never been trained or mentored in being loyal, faithful, and submitted to authority. When something does not go their way, they simply quit. I know you may feel that the job you are in is not taking you anywhere, but God knows you are there. Instead of complaining about that job, you should do all you can, do your best, and help your company make money. God will make a way for you when He finds you faithful. Staying submitted and loyal will pay off in big dividends in your life.

Every year Jesus' parents went to Jerusalem for the Festival of the Passover. When he was twelve years old, they went up to the festival, according to the custom. After the festival was over, while his parents were returning home, the boy Jesus stayed behind in Jerusalem, but they were unaware of it. Think-

ing he was in their company, they traveled on for a day. Then they began looking for him among their relatives and friends. When they did not find him, they went back to Jerusalem to look for him. After three days they found him in the temple courts, sitting among the teachers, listening to them and asking them questions. Everyone who heard him was amazed at his understanding and his answers. When his parents saw him, they were astonished. His mother said to him, "Son, why have you treated us like this? Your father and I have been anxiously searching for you."

"Why were you searching for me?" he asked. "Didn't you know I had to be in my Father's house?" But they did not understand what he was saying to them.

Then he went down to Nazareth with them and was obedient to them. *But his mother treasured all these things in her heart.* ***And Jesus grew in wisdom and stature, and in favor with God and man.***

—Luke 2:41-52

The Amplified Version says it this way: "*He went down to Nazareth with them, and was continually submissive and obedient to them; and His mother treasured all these things in her heart.*"

I mean He is Jesus, right? If anyone belonged in the temple, it would be Him, right? No, wrong. That was not where He was supposed to be. At that point in his life, He was supposed to be with his father and helping in the family business. By submitting to them, the Bible says He "*grew in wisdom and stature, and in favor with God and man.*"

I have trained sales reps for over 35 years and have watched people and had them surprise me. On the one hand, I have hired people that told me how great they were, yet they were big flops in business. On the other hand, I have hired people that I really had second thoughts about coming on board, and they became great at sales and made big money. The difference was that they were submitted to the process and stayed with it until they became good at it. This is God's way of promotion, friend.

I hated school growing up. I barely graduated from high school with a 1.3 average. I think I missed more classes than I attended. I am not proud of that, but that is where I was at. After God called me to preach when I was 19, the first thing He told me to do was to go to college. I thought, *Oh, my gosh; you have got to be kidding.* That was the last thing I wanted to do. He also told me to go to Oral Roberts University. It had a high grade average requirement to be accepted, which I did not have. Then, of course, it was not cheap; and I did not have the money either. I prayed about it, because I had to know for sure I was hearing God. And over and over again, I felt I was to go. I did have one thing going for me. After getting saved, I attended a small Bible school for one year after high school and earned straight A's. I was hoping that would have some influence on their decision. So, I sent in my application and the transcripts from high school and the one year of Bible school.

I can remember when I got the call from the admittance officer. The first thing she said was, "You probably know, Gary, that ORU has a very high grade point average requirement to be considered to attend, which you do not have." I said I knew that. Then she said, "But I notice that you got straight A's in this Bible school you attended for one year. Can you explain why the change?" I then went on to tell her how I was born again and how God had called me to preach. She asked a few more questions and then said, "Well, Gary, I am going to make an exception in your case and approve your application."

Wow, I was thrilled and scared at the same time. I had saved some money but not enough to pay for college. Amazingly, my dad came to me and said he would pay the difference. So that fall, I headed into the unknown. I had never lived away from home before, had never driven out of state before, and had basically flunked out of high school. I can remember the day I put my clothes in my little Fiat 850 coupe and headed out.

To make a long story short, college was harder than I had ever dreamed it would be. Especially since I had really skipped a lot of my high school classes. In the first year at ORU, English was a required class, and during that class, I was required to write a paper. I did my best and thought I did fairly well, but when I got it back from my professor, it had a big red F on the front; and below that, it said, "Is it possible that you even went to high school?" I had to have a tutor for most of that year, to make it through, and ended up with a C average for the year. Which, by the way, I was thrilled about as it was much better than the D's and F's I had received in high school.

But college was the hardest thing I had ever done up until that point in my life. Just getting to college was challenging. Besides getting accepted and having to leave home, I had a major hurdle to pass when I arrived on campus. I was shocked that in my acceptance letter there was a note from the admittance office stating that they had noticed I was overweight. ORU was known for their stance on physical fitness and keeping the human body healthy. The note went on to say that my acceptance into the school was dependent on me losing 15 pounds before I arrived. In fact, before I could register, the very first thing I was to do upon arriving at campus was to report to the gym to be weighed. I know today that policy would not fly, but in 1977, that was their requirement.

Wow. My family was in the pizza business. Of course, I was overweight. I had no idea how to lose weight, so I went out and bought a pair of tennis shoes and started running, but I had such bad shin splints that I had to stop. So, I cut back on my eating and rode my bike during the summer; and when I arrived on campus, I made my goal by one pound.

When I was going through college, I thought there could be nothing harder than college. But I was wrong. After college, God called me into business selling life insurance. I argued and argued with God about that, but that is where He wanted me to be. Many of my friends called me and told me I was missing God as God had called me to preach, with a very dramatic vision, when I was 19. I knew I was called to preach!

It was during this time that I met Drenda, the love of my life! We were engaged to be married during this time when God was dealing with me to go into business. On the trip to Georgia to ask her father for her hand in marriage, I attended her home church on Sunday. A lady walked up to me there and said she had a word for me. At the time, that concept was pretty new to me, but she told me I was looking at a job, and the Lord gave me nine points about this job. She then went on to describe the job I had been looking at in great detail, every point accurately describing the position I was looking at. She ended her word she had for me with, "The Lord said to take the job. Do not be afraid; He is in it." So that was that. I will have to say, I was a bit stunned by her accuracy but was even more relieved that I then knew what to do.

I went back and started working in that job. I thought college was hard, but it seemed easy compared to what I had to do in that new position. I was selling life insurance, and I was paid on a purely commission basis. Most of my business was from cold-calling, which I dreaded. I will admit that I died a million deaths in that job. I dreamed of quitting almost every day. But I had a pastor in Tulsa who said that once you hear direction from God, you stay there until God says to move. So, I stayed there. If I had not have had that confirmation from the Spirit of God at Drenda's church, I probably would have quit. Since I knew God put me there, where could I go? No, I had to remain faithful and stay submitted. Eventually, I became good at talking to people, and my office became the largest office out of 5,000 offices in the United States with one of the vendors I worked with.

It was at this point that God said for me to start a church and teach people about His Kingdom. Start a church? I did not know how to do that. Again, it was hard, and again, I wanted to quit many times. But I stayed with it. Then God called me to do TV, and that was definitely one of the hardest things I had ever done.

What I am trying to say is this. You must persevere and **stay under authority**, even if you do not like it, especially if you do not like it. God

GOD IS ALLOWING YOU TO BE STRETCHED AND YOUR CAPACITY TO BE ENLARGED FOR THE ASSIGNMENT HE HAS FOR YOU DOWN THE ROAD.

is allowing you to be stretched and your capacity to be enlarged for the assignment He has for you down the road. Your loyalty and submission will be tested. Promotion will come at the right season, and God will open the doors for you. The process of being faithful when sometimes you do not like what you are doing, and no one knows your name, is the primary training ground for leadership in a kingdom as well as in a corporation. Remember, there are positions that you don't necessarily call yourself to. God will lead you along the journey. He knows the destiny He has planned for you.

God wants to trust you with an assignment, but you must qualify for it. In our culture, everyone wants to start at the top and bypass God's promotion system. Just remember that staying submitted to God means staying submitted in your heart to God, and, of course, that means staying submitted to those He has placed over you as well. Stay in your lane. God will tell you when it is time to move.

CHAPTER
FIVE

NO
FEAR

Let' take a moment to look at a brief review: You are called to occupy. To occupy is less about power and more about authority and administration, specifically delegated authority. Remember, power follows authority, and because of that, Satan's number one mission is to destroy authority, to tear down those who are in authority. In today's culture, we see that everywhere we look. Men, God's leaders of families, are attacked and belittled in the media. In most family shows, the father appears as a weak, goofy follower of a strong woman. Defunding the police is the cry on the streets, and the Constitution, the bedrock of authority over our great nation, is under attack.

> TO OCCUPY IS LESS ABOUT POWER AND MORE ABOUT AUTHORITY AND ADMINISTRATION, SPECIFICALLY DELEGATED AUTHORITY.

This is where the battle is, friend. Satan wants to tear down every political and CEO position in this country. Why? Because he is after authority. He has lusted after authority since the days of Adam and Eve. He wanted their authority, and he wants your authority. Adam and Eve had complete authority over Satan in the Garden, but he was able to talk them out of it. In the same way, in Christ, you have complete authority over him. Are you going to let him talk you out of it?

The fact of the matter is most believers do not know they have complete authority over Satan; they are afraid of him. I am telling you the truth. Most believers today are afraid of the devil. I heard one woman say that she was done trying to step out into the ideas that God gives her, because every time she does, all hell breaks loose. Well, guess what? You are anointed and have been given the authority to deal with hell.

Let me say this again very clearly: Jesus did not say to conquer the devil but to occupy. The battle is over! The devil is completely and totally defeated. You will never be able to occupy what God has called you to occupy if you are in fear of what the devil can do to you. Let's also remember that to occupy means to fill a space, a territory, or position and to use your authority to maintain occupation of it. Again, we occupy by administering justice, God's laws. This is not a battle we fight but rather is legal enforcement of the victory Jesus won.

Think of a courtroom. Two opposing parties bring their viewpoints to the judge, who hears the case and gives a verdict based on the prevailing law. There is no fight, no wrestling with the opponent. It is a legal matter. If the losing party disagrees and refuses to yield, the government will then step in with power to enforce the decision.

This is how we are to occupy; it is a legal issue. But sadly, most Christians do not understand their legal standing or how to stand up to the devil's challenges. They yield out of fear or intimidation. When facing a challenge, they will run to Google instead of the Word of God. When making a decision about how to live, they will go to social media and the culture to render a decision.

The Bible says the following, *"Put on the full armor of God, so that you can take your stand against the devil's schemes"* (Ephesians 6:11). The devil's schemes! He has no power, no authority, only lies and schemes. We will dig into Ephesians 6 later in this chapter, but first, I need to make sure you understand this most important fact:

We are not at war with Satan!

It is imperative that you know this. We are not at war with Satan. We are in conflict with him but only in a legal sense. If we say he is at war with the church, the term war implies that the battle is not over, the victory is still undecided. The concept that Satan and the church are at war implies he has the power to wage war. **HE DOES NOT!** I know what you are thinking, *Well, Gary, it sure feels like it sometimes.* I understand that, but we are not led by our feelings. Again, this is a legal issue, not a feeling issue. For instance, you do not need to feel like you are a citizen to be a citizen of the United States. I do not have to feel like I own the car I drive. No, these are all legal issues that are easily proven in a court of law if questioned. So, when dealing with the devil, do not let him drag you into an emotional discussion!

Satan has no legal jurisdiction over you! None!

> *For he has rescued us from the dominion of darkness and brought us into the kingdom of the Son he loves.*
> —Colossians 1:13

Jesus has brought us out of Satan's legal jurisdiction into the Kingdom of God. Satan has no say whatsoever concerning the laws of our Kingdom. But that will not stop him from trying. He will test you with thoughts that tend to challenge what God's laws say. It is only your knowledge of your legal rights as a citizen of God's Kingdom that will keep you safe from Satan's lies and deception. Everything rests on your response to his challenges. Can you call his bluff? As a citizen, you have legal rights!

> *Consequently, you are no longer foreigners and strangers, but fellow **citizens** with God's people and also members of his household.*
> —Ephesians 2:19

I was riding my bike one morning, which I try to do three or four times a week when the weather permits. I have several routes I take, depending on how long I want to ride. The route I take the most is a 16-mile ride through the beautiful farmland of Knox County, Ohio. I have ridden on this route for over 20 years. I know every dog on that route, and they know me. But this one morning, there was a new dog, and he was coming toward me, running as fast as he could. His teeth were snapping as he ran toward my spinning pedals. I was a little shocked by it all since I was not expecting him. I kicked my speed into high gear and was able to stay just ahead of his snapping teeth. Wow, I realized that dog meant business, and it made me reevaluate whether I should take that route for a while. But I knew better. Why would I let a dog run me off of my favorite route to ride? I pay my taxes, and I have a legal right to ride there.

From previous experience with dogs, I knew how to handle it the next time he came out. This method does take some courage, but it works. The next day I took the same ride, and sure enough, here he came, teeth snapping and barking fiercely. But this time, instead of speeding up, I slowed down and waited, which allowed the dog to come out into the road in front of me. This was right where I wanted him. He seemed a little confused and slowed down. At this point, I aimed my bike directly at him and yelled, "NO!" with a loud, authoritative voice. I then pointed my arm toward his house and yelled again, "NO!" The dog stopped and then slowly walked off the road about 20 feet into his yard and just stood there as I slowly passed by.

I pass this dog every time I ride, but now, he rarely gets up to see me. Actually, he has become my friend and wags his tail when I come by. Here is what I know. That dog lives with a family. I assume that they are not going to own a dog that would treat them that way. I also assume that they correct him from time to time. They are his alpha dog, so to speak.

So, if I act like I have authority over dogs, usually, they will back down. Now, I am not suggesting that you should just walk into their master's yard. That would provoke their protective instinct. But on the road, they usually back down. "What is the reason you aim your bike at them?" you ask. If a loud "No" does not work, I speed up right toward the dog and start yelling. That always does it. The motto of the story is you are in charge. Don't let the dog or the devil bluff you out of your legal rights.

Satan has no ability to wage war!

> *And having **disarmed** the powers and authorities, he made a public spectacle of them, triumphing over them by the cross.*
> —Colossians 2:15

Did you read that? Jesus made a spectacle of the devil!

The word spectacle means: Something exhibited to view as unusual, notable, or entertaining, especially an eye-catching or dramatic public display: an object of contempt.[9]

But, Gary, the Bible says we have an enemy. Yes, but also remember that he is a defeated enemy. Well, Gary, Paul calls the devil our enemy in 1 Peter 5:8:

> *Be alert and of sober mind. Your enemy the devil prowls around like a roaring lion looking for someone to devour.*

9. https://www. merriam-webster.com/spectacle

Stop! Read the text. The devil is looking for someone to devour. He has no legal jurisdiction to devour just anyone he wants to devour. Peter said the devil roams around like a roaring lion. What does the lion's roar do in the jungle? It invokes fear. Fear opens the door to the enemy because it is unbelief. But Peter gives you the answer in the first part of the Scripture. Be alert and sober minded. That Greek word for sober means to be **calm and collected in spirit**.[10] So when the devil roars, you stay calm with your thoughts controlled by the knowledge that you have complete dominion over him. Scientists say a lion roars to scare off intruders and to show dominance.[11] So, let me paraphrase why he roars: to invoke fear, to say he is in charge, to affirm his dominance, to cause his enemies to back down.

> SO WHEN THE DEVIL ROARS, YOU STAY CALM WITH YOUR THOUGHTS CONTROLLED BY THE KNOWLEDGE THAT YOU HAVE COMPLETE DOMINION OVER HIM.

What Peter was saying is when the devil roars, do not panic, do not back down. Stay calm and collected, know your legal rights, and stand on them.

> *The commander ordered that Paul be taken into the barracks. He directed that he be flogged and interrogated in order to find out why the people were shouting at him like this. As they stretched him out to flog him, Paul said to the centurion standing there. "Is it legal for you to flog a Roman citizen who*

10. https://biblehub.com/greek/3525.htm
11. James Ball, "Why Do Lions Roar? (4 Reasons Why)," https://www.wildlife boss.com, August 4, 2022.

hasn't even been found guilty? When the centurion heard this, he went to the commander and reported it. "What are you going to do?" he asked. "This man is a Roman citizen."

The commander went to Paul and asked, "Tell me, are you a Roman citizen?" "Yes, I am," he answered. Then the commander said, "I had to pay a lot of money for my citizenship." "But I was born a citizen," Paul replied. Those who were about to interrogate him __*withdrew immediately*__*. The commander himself was alarmed when he realized that he had put Paul, a Roman citizen, in chains.*

—Acts 22:24-29

If you are going to deal with the devil, you must know your legal rights. He will always bluff you with the lie that you do not have legal rights over him. That is when you pull out the sword of the Spirit and let him have it.

Here is our stance against the devil and his demons.

The seventy-two returned with joy and said, "Lord, even the demons submit to us in your name."

He replied, "I saw Satan fall like lightning from heaven. I have given you __*authority*__ *to trample on snakes and scorpions and to overcome all the power of the enemy; nothing will harm you. However, do not rejoice that the spirits submit to you, but rejoice that your names are written in heaven.*

—Luke 10:17-20

Some versions say, "Nothing shall by any means harm you!"

I love this Scripture. It lays out clearly that you are the one who has the authority here, not the roaring lion. Please catch this important truth. You have been given authority to trample on snakes and scorpions and all the power of the enemy. To trample on them means you pay no attention to them. They are nothing under your feet! In my daily life, I am sure that I trample on insects without knowing it. I give them no thought. Instead, my thoughts are focused on where I am headed, what I am doing. In the same way, Jesus is saying, "Do not give thought to the devil and demons. They are nothing to your authority! Go about your Kingdom assignment, and do not allow yourself to be distracted."

> *And these signs will accompany those who believe: In my name they will drive out demons; they will speak in new tongues; they will pick up snakes with their hands; and when they drink deadly poison, it will not hurt them at all; they will place their hands on sick people, and they will get well.*
>
> —Mark 16:17-18

Notice this is the directive given to the church. "Go, and these signs will accompany you: You can cast out demons. You can pick up a snake with your hands, and it will not hurt you. If you drink poison, it will not hurt you. You can place your hands on sick people, and you will not get sick. They will get well!"

Do you see it? The devil has no authority over you!

Now, if you're afraid of that snake, if he convinces you to be afraid, you'll never go in there and set people free.

"But, Gary, Paul said we are in warfare, didn't he?" Yes, he did, but who or what are we fighting against? Let's take a look at that Scripture.

The weapons we fight with are not the weapons of the world. On the contrary, they have divine power to demolish strongholds. We demolish arguments and every pretension that sets itself up against the knowledge of God, and we take captive every thought to make it obedient to Christ.

—2 Corinthians 10:4-5

The King James Version says it this way:

For the weapons of our warfare are not carnal, but mighty through God to the pulling down of strong holds; casting down imaginations, and every high thing that exalteth itself against the knowledge of God, and bringing into captivity every thought to the obedience of Christ.

What is the warfare over?

What are the strongholds he is talking about? Are they demons? No, he is talking about preconceived ideas or pretensions that have set themselves up against the knowledge of God. I am sure you have met people who have said, "Well, I just do not believe like that." Now, if you handed them your Bible and asked them to show you what they believe and why they believe what they are saying, they usually cannot tell you. They have been taught something from someone in the past, and what they were told has become their truth. They are not open to a different idea. They have become, as they say, closed-minded. Their perception has now become a stronghold. Their wrong and untrue thoughts have locked out truth. So, in this battle then, who is the prisoner? Is it Satan and his demons? Is that who we are looking to arrest and lock up?

"...*and **we take captive every thought** to make it obedient to Christ.*"

No, thoughts contrary to God's truth are the enemy, not Satan. The weapons of our warfare are God's thoughts, His truth. They eliminate everything false and tear down strongholds. The warfare is over what we believe!

Let's take a look at Ephesians 6 for a closer look as to how this works.

> *Finally, be strong in the Lord and in his mighty power. Put on the full armor of God, so that you can take your stand against the devil's schemes. For our **struggle** is not against flesh and blood, but against the rulers, against the authorities, against the powers of this dark world and against the spiritual forces of the evil in the heavenly realms. Therefore, put on the full armor of God, so that when the day of evil comes, you may be able to stand your ground, and after you have done everything to stand.*
>
> *Stand firm then, with the belt of truth buckled around your waist, with the breastplate of righteousness in place, and with your feet fitted with the readiness that comes from the gospel of peace. In addition to all this, take up the shield of faith, with which you can extinguish all the flaming arrows of the evil one. Take the helmet of salvation and the sword of the Spirit, which is the word of God. And pray in the Spirit on all occasions with all kinds of prayers and requests.*
>
> —Ephesians 6:10-18a

Okay, what is Paul talking about and what is our armor? First of all, he mentions the belt of truth. Obviously, the truth he is talking about is God's Word. If you think of the purpose of a belt today, it is to hold your pants up. Well, the belt which was part of

YOU HAVE GOD'S TRUTH THAT YOU HAVE BEEN MADE RIGHTEOUS IN CHRIST JESUS.

the Roman armor in those days was to hold up the breastplate. The breastplate would be latched and sitting on the belt of truth. So, in this case, the breastplate of righteousness would be God's truth concerning your righteousness in Christ. It would protect you from any condemning thoughts the enemy may throw at you. You have God's truth that you have been made righteous in Christ Jesus. Knowing the truth, you simply cast those condemning thoughts down as untrue. Your feet fitted with the readiness that comes from the gospel of peace can best be explained by looking at Proverbs 4.

Let your eyes look straight ahead; fix your gaze directly before you. Give careful thought to the paths for your feet and be steadfast in all your ways. Do not turn to the right or the left; keep your foot from evil.

—Proverbs 4:25-27

Simply put, stay out of the devil's territory. Make straight paths for your feet. Pursue righteousness. The shield of faith, of course, is being in full agreement and believing the Word of God, which is called faith. Faith immediately rejects any thought that does not line up with God's Word. When a circumstance or a thought tries to lie to you, faith immediately responds with, "It is written." The helmet of salvation is simply thinking God's thoughts.

You will keep in perfect peace those whose minds are steadfast, because they trust in you.

—Isaiah 26:3

The sword of the Spirit is the Word of God and can be used in both a defensive posture and in an offensive posture. It has the ability to slice through deception and then also to bring the power of God's Word into any situation that needs it. Praying in the Spirit is to enable you to receive thoughts from the Spirit of God regarding supernatural strategies or needed knowledge.

If you look at <u>every piece of armor</u> mentioned, they all deal with only one thing: what we believe and what we think. <u>None of it mentions attacking the devil.</u> All of it is spoken of as being in a defensive position, except the sword of the Spirit and praying in the Spirit, which can go into an offensive mode as well as defensive. Paul tells us to put our armor on because we struggle against these spiritual forces.

The word for struggle here actually means to wrestle. Let me give you the Strong's definition for that word wrestle:

> Wrestle: a contest between two in which each endeavors to throw the other, and which is decided when the victor is able to hold his opponent down with his hand upon his neck.[12]

What is the wrestling match over? Thoughts! Which thoughts are you going to believe? Which thoughts are you going to allow to have dominance, and which ones are you going to throw off?

12. James Strong, *Strong's Exhaustive Concordance of the Bible*, Hendrickson Publishers.

YOU HAVE BEEN PROGRAMMED BY THE WORLD'S UPSIDE-DOWN, PERVERSE, AND UNBELIEVING CULTURE. WE ALL HAVE; WE GREW UP HERE.

Again, think of a wrestling match. Someone is going to end up on top. Many times, we are dealing with a pattern of thought that we have been raised with and do not even recognize its danger. This is why Paul says in Romans 12:

Do not conform to the pattern of this world but be transformed by the renewing of your mind. Then **you will be able to test and approve what God's will is, his good, pleasing and perfect will.**

—Romans 12:2

When Paul is talking about the pattern of this world, he is talking about your thoughts. You have been programmed by the world's upside-down, perverse, and unbelieving culture. We all have; we grew up here. There is a wrestling match between God's Word and what you have been taught in the culture. Both are trying to obtain dominance, and the one that wins, the one that you hold on to will determine if Satan has any legal ground in your life. Paul makes it clear that we need to put on this armor, meaning we need to take the time to know what God says to be able to discern the lies from the enemy or strongholds we may have that stand in agreement with Satan. We are to cast down imaginations that exalt themselves over God's truth. Again, Paul says if we know the truth, we will be able to take our stand against the devil's schemes. We can say, "No, that is not true," and we can stand on the Word of God in the day of trouble.

I remember on a very wintery day in Ohio, my boys wanted to

go out to the back hill to sled. I do not remember why I told them that I did not want them to do that, but that was my answer. Well, I guess they could not resist, disobeyed, and went out anyway. It wasn't that long until I heard Tom crying hysterically as he came into the house with blood all over his face. One tooth was hanging by a thread. The story goes that as they were going down the hill on the metal sled, he hit a bump. Apparently, Tom was lying facedown on the sled when it hit the bump. The bump caused his mouth to smash down on the metal frame of the sled and hit his front teeth. Well, it was a mess.

We left immediately for our dentist, who was about 20 minutes from our house. We asked him to look at Tom's tooth and if he could put the tooth back in. As he was examining Tom's mouth, we were shocked to hear the dentist say that not only did he have the tooth that was dangling, but also there was a tooth missing. A tooth missing? The dentist told us that we needed to go on to Children's Hospital where they could examine his mouth and see if his tooth could be saved. We then asked him about the missing tooth. Could it be put back in? He told us that it would rarely work, but there was a possibility it could, a very slim one, and that was if we could find the tooth quickly enough for it to have a chance. Find the tooth? The snow was a foot deep, and the tooth was white. That could be difficult. This was a moment where we had to choose what we would believe. In the wrestling match in our minds, one thought would prevail: the dentist's, which said it was almost impossible for that tooth to be reattached, or what we said about it in agreement with God's Word.

Truly I tell you, if anyone says to this mountain, "Go, throw yourself into the sea," and does not doubt in their heart but believes that what they say will happen, it will be done for them.

—Mark 11:23

We chose God's Word and then were faced with finding the tooth. Tom's brother, Tim, was at home, and we sent him out to look for the tooth in the deep snow. We prayed in agreement that he would find it. About an hour later, we received a call from Amy, Tom's older sister, that the tooth had indeed been found. The doctor had told us that if by chance we did find the tooth, it should be put in milk and brought to the hospital as quickly as possible. By then, we were downtown at the hospital and faced another problem. Tim and the kids were home, and they had no milk to put the tooth in. They also had no way to drive the tooth to the hospital. So, we gave Tim instructions to go and ask the neighbor for some milk, and we called a friend to go to the house and drive the tooth to the hospital.

The dentist at the hospital was even more negative than the dentist we first saw, for a couple of reasons. It had been hours then since the tooth had not been in his mouth, and secondly, the tooth may have become damaged in the accident and cracked. Finally, the tooth arrived at the hospital, and, amazingly, it was not cracked. The dentist put the tooth in place but said it would probably not last. Well, that was almost 20 years ago, and Tom's front teeth are still perfect. The tooth that fell out did not yellow or turn grey as the dentist said it would. It is just as white as the other tooth.

WHEN CIRCUMSTANCES SPEAK, YOU MUST SPEAK LOUDER!

YOU MUST ANSWER EVERY LIE! WHEN CIRCUM-STANCES SPEAK, YOU MUST SPEAK LOUDER!

What was Satan's strategy with Adam and Eve?

> *Did God really say, "You must not eat from any tree in the garden"?*
>
> —Genesis 3:1b

Notice how the devil always gets part of it right but leaves out just enough to snare you if you do not know the truth of God's Word. Notice he said, "You cannot eat from any tree in the garden." Well, of course, that was not true. God had said they could eat from any tree in the Garden, but:

> *"You must not eat from the tree of the knowledge of good and evil, for when you eat from it you will certainly die."*
>
> —Genesis 2:16a–17

If you have your armor on and you know the truth, he will not want to mess with you.

> *You believe that there is one God. You do well. Even the demons believe—and **tremble**.*
>
> —James 2:19 (NKJV)

> *Submit yourselves, then to God. Resist the devil, and he will **flee from you**.*
>
> —James 4:7

How do we resist? In our own strength? Of course not. This is when you pull out the sword of the Spirit while making sure all your armor is ready with God's truth.

The word flee in the Greek means: to flee away, to seek safety by flight, to shun or avoid something abhorrent by fleeing, to flee from danger.[13]

No, he will not want to mess with you then, because he will know that you have absolute authority over him.

Yes, you do!

13. https://biblehub.com/greek/5343.htm

PEOPLE, YOUR ANSWER OR YOUR PROBLEM: PART ONE

Most of the time when we talk about being in conflict with the devil or demons, we are usually talking about dealing with the devil's people. A demon is not usually wanting to show itself as it knows that once you realize it is there, you will deal with it. No, our biggest struggle in occupying the territory that God gives us to occupy is dealing with demon-inspired people or putting the wrong people in the wrong box of responsibility.

You will need people where you are headed. That is why God will take some time to train you by having you work with or for people to gain wisdom in this area. I would have to say, most of the problems—and quite frankly, the biggest problems—I have had in my ministry and business have been people related. Then again, the biggest victories I have had in ministry and business have been because of people. So, who are you going to put in that organizational chart when you need a job done? Who has the character and the ability to occupy that space? Big questions. And you need to get it right. And I will admit, it is hard, but if we follow some good, sound principles of discernment, we can do pretty well.

In my opinion, the first and most important quality to look for in anyone you put in a place of delegated authority is that they **MUST** understand how a kingdom works! How authority flows down from the head of the organization, who they report to, and who reports to them. They must have passed the submission test long ago and must have proven loyalty.

Satan is going to try to break the chain of command, and he will look for the weakest link in your structure. Remember, authority flows from the head down, and power follows authority. Satan is going to try to insert himself into your organizational chart; and, yes, there will be a name attached to it. His goal is to stop the flow of power that is intersecting his kingdom here on earth. And he is going to try to deceive people out of their positions or lure people into positions that are not theirs to take.

You must be sure that when someone down the line speaks, they are speaking your words, not theirs. For instance, now that you understand Kingdom law, in the past, if I sent someone to the hospital to pray for a person, they would often hear this, "Well, I thought Pastor Gary was coming." But what they did not understand was I was there. See, we have not been taught this. "No, I want Pastor Gary to come." As I told you, I was there. I gave this person my delegated authority, which means I gave them my authority, my anointing, my grace. They had my grace, the same grace I would have had if I were there.

Jesus said, "If you've seen me, you've seen the Father." Exactly! If I send someone in my name, they should speak the same thing I would have spoken if I were there. But see, we've not been taught that, have we? Especially in our American culture, we've not been taught that. But this is how a kingdom works.

THE ISSUE IN OUR CHURCHES IS OUR SPECTATOR STYLE OF CHRISTIANITY WE WERE TAUGHT GROWING UP.

When we were a smaller church and I had not taught the people how a kingdom works, I heard this kind of comment quite often. "Pastor Gary needs to do this or do that." After I taught my church the truth and instructed them on how a kingdom works and how authority flows down from the head, most of that stopped.

The issue in our churches is our spectator style of Christianity we were taught growing up. I grew up in a denominational church, and the church I grew up in had a pastor and a secretary that volunteered during the week. That is all. That was it. The pastor did everything. It was his responsibility to do all the weddings, all the funerals, go to the hospital, pray for the sick, and the list went on and on. I can remember hearing my dad complaining about the pastor not visiting someone. He would say, "The pastor should have visited that person; that is why we pay a pastor." And that is what people have been taught and what they have seen as an example: It is the pastor's job. We were never taught that we, the normal everyday church members, have authority to do the works of Jesus.

When Paul was teaching Pastor Timothy, who pastored the church in Ephesus, how to pick leaders, he said to look at the person's homelife. We talked about this in a previous chapter. We said if you look at a person's homelife, it will tell you a lot about what that person will duplicate in your organization.

I have a friend who is a pastor of a large church, and when he started out, he needed to hire a few people. So, he did the typical thing people do when looking for an employee. He gathered up some resumes, talked to those that applied, and made some hires. Sadly, the people he hired did not work out. It seemed that what was written on their resumes did not match the level of excellence that he wanted, so he let them go and tried again, with the same result. Again, he had to let them go. After analyzing what went wrong, he realized there was a flaw in his hiring procedure: the resumes were not telling the whole story, and neither were the applicants.

So, he changed how he interviewed his candidates. After the resume review, which he found out meant almost nothing, he would ask the candidate to walk him to their car in the parking lot. He wanted to see how well kept and clean the car was. If there were french fries smashed into the carpet, empty coke bottles and trash all through the car, then he knew if he hired that person, his church would end up looking like their car. He even went a step further in his investigation. He would stop by their home unannounced in the evening. Same thing. If all the wallpaper was falling off the walls and there was trash all around the house, again, he knew what his church would look like if they were hired. He said after he started to hire based on this method, he found the people of excellence he was looking for. But the most important thing he looked at was how the family functioned.

Paul told Timothy the most important thing to observe in a candidate was not just a clean house but to look for respect and honor in the family. Paul knew that the family is a mini organizational chart. If the father could not properly exercise authority and training there, he knew that there was no way he would have the ability to manage a larger organization like the church.

TODAY, PEOPLE ARE ALL CAUGHT UP WITH TITLES. BUT HAVING A TITLE DOES NOT MAKE A PERSON QUALIFIED FOR A PLACE OF AUTHORITY!

Today, people are all caught up with titles. But having a title does not make a person qualified for a place of authority! I have made mistakes in putting people in positions too many times. In the end, it always cost me money and lost time. I remember when we needed to hire a person to work in our TV department. We put out ads with the job description we were hiring for along with the qualifications needed to accomplish the job.

A woman answered the ad and came to us with a great resume.

She had worked for a large ministry in a high management position running their TV department and had just left, she said, because the ministry was downsizing their staff. Well, it did not take long before I became suspicious. She did not know what she was doing—at all! I found out through some digging that she never actually worked in a TV department but had only been a writer, and, no, they were not downsizing. They had fired her. So, when you are looking for someone to fill a spot on your occupation team, remind yourself to look past the flattery and the great talent and to look at their track record in regard to loyalty and submission.

In 1 Corinthians chapter 3, Paul is teaching the church in Corinth along this same topic, and he says the following:

> *Brothers and sisters, I could not address you as people who live by the Spirit but as people who are still worldly—mere infants in Christ. I gave you milk, not solid food, for you were not yet ready for it. Indeed, you are still not ready. You are still worldly. For since there is jealousy and quarreling among you, are you not worldly? Are you not acting like mere humans? For when one says, "I follow Paul," and another, "I follow Apollos," are you not mere human beings? What, after all, is Apollos? And what is Paul? Only servants, through whom you came to believe—as the Lord has assigned to each his task. I planted the seed, Apollos watered it, but God has been making it grow.*
>
> *So neither the one who plants nor the one who waters is anything, but only God, who makes things grow. The one who plants and the one who waters have one purpose, and they will each be rewarded according to their own labor. For we are co-workers in God's service; you are God's field, God's building. By the grace God has given me, I laid a foundation as a wise*

builder, and someone else is building on it. But each one should build with care. For no one can lay any foundation other than the one already laid, which is Jesus Christ.

—1 Corinthians 3:1-11

In verse 1, he says, *"Brothers and sisters, I could not address you as people who live by the Spirit but as people who are still worldly—mere infants in Christ. I gave you milk, not solid food, for you were not yet ready for it."* What does a baby do with solid food? They spit it out, or they change churches. I wish I was kidding, but I'm just telling you how it is.

He goes on, *"Indeed, you are still not ready. You are still worldly. For since there is jealousy and quarreling among you, are you not worldly?"* Jealousy and quarreling over what? Position. Visibility. Who's more spiritual than someone else.

Are you not acting like mere humans? For when one says, "I follow Paul," and another, "I follow Apollos," are you not mere human beings? What, after all, is Apollos? And what is Paul? Only servants, through whom you came to believe—as the Lord has assigned to each his task. I planted the seed, Apollos watered it, but God has been making it grow.

—1 Corinthians 3:3b-6

What is God interested in? God is interested in growth. And these people are all out of order, all enamored with what glitters or gets the most attention. They have lost sight of the plan of God, that each person has their own giftings and assignment, and God has given each of them grace for that assignment. Why? So, everything would grow as each part does its part. Paul knew that if the church would operate in order, honoring each other's gifts and callings, things would grow!

> *So neither the one who plants nor the one who waters is anything, but only God, who makes things grow. The one who plants and the one who waters have **one purpose**, and they will each be rewarded according to their own labor. For we are co-workers in God's service; you are God's field, God's building.*
>
> ***By the grace God has given me**, I laid a foundation as a wise builder.*
>
> —1 Corinthians 3:7-10a

Another version of the Bible says it this way:

> ***By the grace God has given me**, I laid a foundation as an expert builder.*
>
> —1 Corinthians 3:10a (BSB)

SEE, EVERYONE HAS GRACE. EVERY ASSIGNMENT HAS GOD'S EMPOWERMENT WITH IT. AND ONE OF THE PLOTS THE ENEMY USES AGAINST YOU IS TO PULL YOU OUT OF THAT GRACE.

Paul tells the church that he is able to work with an excellent ability by God's grace. He recognizes that the grace he walks in is for a specific purpose and position and is encouraging those in that church to find their places. See, everyone has grace. Every assignment has God's empowerment with it. And one of the plots the enemy uses against you is to pull you out of that grace.

For instance, I am not administrative. If I must deal with administrative things very long, my brain begins to get tired. But it's amazing. I have people on staff who love administration. They love it, love it, love it. And I think, *That's weird. How can you love administration?* The Bible says He gives people different giftings, He assigns people to different tasks. When they are in their gifting, they love it. It actually energizes them. So, here's what the enemy wants to do. He wants to pull you out of your grace.

Now, I can teach all day, because I am passionate about the Kingdom. I love teaching the Kingdom. I can teach all day. At the end of the day, I'll be tired, but I'll be enthusiastic. I'll have more energy at the end of the day than I do at the beginning of the day, because I'm in my grace. I am in my gifting. But you know what it feels like when you're outside of your grace, right? You need to take a nap!

You might have friends that call you and dump all their problems on you, and you know what that feels like, right? You see they have the grace to raise their own families, but when they try to let you take responsibility for the bills they can't pay or the problems they are dealing with, it pulls you outside of your grace and pulls the energy right out of you.

THE ENEMY LOVES TO DRAW YOU OUT OF YOUR GRACE INTO WHAT IS CALLED FALSE RESPONSIBILITY.

The enemy loves to draw you out of your grace into what is called false responsibility. He wants to drag you into false responsibility that you have no grace for, no empowerment by God for. As people try to give you their responsibility and you try to solve all their problems, you step out of position. You will get worn out, and things will stop growing and working right in your life—you are out of place. Paul is saying here that there's grace for a position, an assignment that God gives you. Stay with that. That is where you will find your strength, passion, and contentment.

Paul continues:

> *Just as a body, though one, has many parts, but all its many parts form one body, so it is with Christ. For we were all baptized by one Spirit so as to form one body—whether Jews or Gentiles, slave or free—and we were all given the one Spirit to drink. Even so the body is not made up of one part but of many.*
>
> *Now if the foot should say, "Because I am not a hand, I do not belong to the body," it would not for that reason stop being part of the body. And if the ear should say, "Because I am not an eye, I do not belong to the body," it would not for that reason stop being part of the body. If the whole body were an eye, where would the sense of hearing be? If the whole body were an ear, where would the sense of smell be? But in fact God has placed the parts in the body, every one of them, just as he wanted them to be. If they were all one part, **where would the body be?** As it is, there are many parts, but one body. The eye cannot say to the hand, "I don't need you!" And the head cannot say to the feet, "I don't need you!"*
>
> —1 Corinthians 12:12-21

Where would the body be?

In a big mess, that's where! Imagine a hand trying to be the eye. You would be totally blind. Imagine if the eye were trying to be a foot. You would not be able to move. You would be blind and disabled! Let me say that again: You would be blind and disabled!

Unfortunately, that is where many pastors and CEOs find their churches or businesses. Nothing grows; everything is in chaos and dysfunction.

> *The eye cannot say to the hand, "I don't need you!" And the head cannot say to the feet, "I don't need you!"*

No, Paul knew that had to be fixed first in Corinth. The church must get in order, or it is isn't going anywhere. The eye must take its created place so that the body can see where it is going, and the foot must take its created place so the body can move forward.

See, the church of Corinth was very immature, right? We already know that. Paul said, "I can't even talk to you as spiritual." In other words, they couldn't even receive a revelation of their assignment yet. They couldn't even receive a revelation of their destiny yet. You know why? Because they couldn't see past themselves. They were all fighting over who was more spiritual, who was getting all the attention. They were even in strife about who the greatest preacher was, Paul or Apollos. They had missed the entire point. It wasn't about Paul or Apollos. It was about God and things growing. They were out of order! In fact, I do not think they even knew there was an order at that point. They were spiritual babies.

So, when we, the body of Christ, want to self-promote ourselves or refuse to stay submitted to where God has assigned us to function, it brings all kinds of problems.

> *For where you have envy and selfish ambition, there **you find disorder** and every evil practice.*
>
> —James 3:16

Once back in the beginning of the church, I had a lady come up to me after a morning prayer meeting, red in the face and angry. In tears, she asked this question, "Why didn't you call on me to pray?" "Was I obligated to call on you to pray?" I asked. "No," she said. I then said to her, "Who's in charge of this meeting? Who has the authority over this meeting? I do."

I didn't tell her she was going to pray. I never even brought it up to her before the meeting that she might be called on to pray. And there she was in tears, "Why didn't you call on me to pray?" So, I said to her, "Because of how you're acting right now is why I did not call on you." See, I knew that she wanted to be seen praying among the ladies; it was an identity thing with her. I also knew that her house was out of order. There was strife between her and her husband. I told her, "You need to pray and ask God to show you why you thought it was so important that you prayed today in the meeting." So, was that lady qualified to be given authority over anything? Absolutely not! She was a baby and an immature person. And as it is with babies, they think they are grown up when they are not.

> **NOW, YOU CAN STAY IN A PLACE OF IMMATURITY, OR YOU CAN CHOOSE TO GROW AND STAY SUBMITTED.**

Now, you can stay in a place of immaturity, or you can choose to grow and stay submitted. I would have liked to say she chose to grow, but she did what a majority of people do when they are coached: she left the church. What she did not understand was that she could change churches, but she would have to pass the same test there.

People that are immature don't realize they're immature.

I believe maturity is not measured by someone's talent, gifting, or age but by their ability to stay submitted when they disagree or are corrected. If you have raised kids, you know that they will beg to do something long before they are mature enough to do it. That is normal with kids, but that is also why they have parents who have wisdom. Now, I'm trying to help you here. I know you want to grow. I know you want to reach your destiny and occupy that place God has ordained you to occupy for Him. But Satan plays on immaturity, and I want to help you avoid his traps, so I need to continue this discussion for a bit longer.

> *Do not let anyone who delights in false humility and the worship of angels **disqualify you**. Such a person also goes into great detail about what they have seen; they are puffed up with idle notions by their unspiritual mind. They have lost connection with the head, from whom the whole body, supported and held together by its ligaments and sinews, grows as God causes it to grow.*
>
> —Colossians 2:18-19

Paul said, *"Do not let anyone who delights in false humility and the worship of angels **disqualify you [for the prize]**."*

First of all, let's be clear. There is a prize, a reward when you fulfill your assignment for God. Paul says you want to make sure that someone else does not disqualify you for that prize. Kind of a strange statement, isn't it? How could someone else disqualify you for your prize? Isn't your prize based on what you do, not on what someone else does? Yes, but what if you never did what you were supposed to do because this other person made you feel so inadequate that you never tried? They made themselves look so spiritual, and you looked at yourself and thought, *I'm nothing. I don't have Words of Knowledge very often. I don't see angels. I don't have dreams every night. Maybe I can't hear God.* So spiritually, you just gave up. You were intimidated by them and viewed yourself in an inferior light. They made you feel that you must yield what you felt was your assignment or position to them since they were so capable. Is this making sense? So, in reality, you disqualified yourself. You no longer saw yourself as qualified in comparison to them. Paul goes on and tells us exactly how this happens.

Such a person goes into great detail about what he or she has seen. And their unspiritual mind puffs them up with idle notions.

Have you ever met a Christian who's always telling you the dream they had last night or how God spoke to them this morning and told them to wear the pink dress instead of the blue one? Their conversations are always about what God showed them, their latest dream, or the amazing time they just had in worship where God showed them this picture or that picture. And let's say God does in fact speak to them at that level and shows them things by the minute. Why do they feel they need to constantly tell you about it? Paul says their minds are filled with idle thoughts. What do those thoughts sound like? *I'm better than you are. I am more spiritual than you are. I should be running that department, or I could have done a better job of teaching that class. Or I can teach better than Pastor. In fact, I should be the pastor of this church.* Here's the deal. Guess what? You're not the pastor of the church. That spot is occupied. And yes, you may in fact teach better than your pastor, but God has not given you that position to occupy.

Paul goes on and says, "These people have lost connection with the head."

Okay, stop everything! We have a problem. How does authority flow? From the head down. But now they see themselves as the authority, the head—but of course they are not. So, what happens next in the church is that person goes to other baby, immature Christians and starts doing what we have just read about in 1 Corinthians 3. They begin to believe puffed up thoughts of their importance. "I should be the hand. I should be the head. I should be the eye." Right? You've heard it.

Here's the thing I want you to understand. The eye was already an eye before it wanted to be a foot. It was created as an eye! God Himself has already created you specifically for Himself with your unique giftings and talents. He has a place for you. He reveals that to us as our character matures and we are able to receive that promotion without saying, "Hey, look at me!"

We need to understand that God will give us assignments. They will start small, but as we are faithful with the little things, we will gain credibility with God and men. We will be promoted by those He has put over us, and He will move us into different assignments as we mature. This is how it works, and there are no shortcuts.

> GOD HIMSELF HAS ALREADY CREATED YOU SPECIFICALLY FOR HIMSELF WITH YOUR UNIQUE GIFTINGS AND TALENTS. HE HAS A PLACE FOR YOU. HE REVEALS THAT TO US AS OUR CHARACTER MATURES.

Because immaturity hides behind talent and flattery. Paul said you need to test anyone you are considering for leadership. Again, test them for what? Talent? No. Their ability to stay submitted. As I have said before, the church is very immature in understanding its role in occupation, which, of course, is what Jesus told us to do. Most of the church is focused on conquering the devil, as I have said, and because of this, has not matured in its understanding and ability to occupy.

Satan wants to stop the flow of power, tear down authority; and many times, he does it through deception. We must always be on guard to see past what may be on the surface of a situation to understand the hidden motives and tactics that the devil may be setting up underground. For instance, I know we have all seen the blue medical insignia that hospitals and health companies use. It is a picture of a pole with a snake on it.

> **SATAN WANTS TO STOP THE FLOW OF POWER, TEAR DOWN AUTHORITY; AND MANY TIMES, HE DOES IT THROUGH DECEPTION.**

They traveled from Mount Hor along the route to the Red Sea, to go around Edom. But the people grew impatient on the way; they spoke against God and against Moses, and said, "Why have you brought us up out of Egypt to die in the wilderness? There is no bread! There is no water! And we detest this miserable food!"

Then the Lord sent venomous snakes among them; they bit the people and many Israelites died. The people came to Moses and said, "We sinned when we spoke against the Lord and against you. Pray that the Lord will take the snakes away from us." So Moses prayed for the people.

The Lord said to Moses, "Make a snake and put it up on a pole; anyone who is bitten can look at it and live." So Moses made a bronze snake and put it up on a pole. Then when anyone was bitten by a snake and looked at the bronze snake, they lived.

—Numbers 21:4-9

So one day, Drenda was reading this, and the Lord said to her: "Do you think that snake on the pole that Moses put up was alive on that pole?" "Of course not," she said. But then God said, "Take a closer look at what your doctors use as their symbol of medical help against disease and death. Is there one snake on that pole?" "No," she said, "there are two." God then said to her, "And are those snakes dead? No! Dead snakes do not curl up a pole. They hang limp."

Wow, I had seen that symbol all my life, and my mind always thought, *That is so great the medical community recognizes that God is the source of life, and they are using the image God gave Israel to signify that the snake, Satan's jurisdiction over their health was dead.* But now I realize, no, that is not a symbol in agreement with God's jurisdiction over Satan. It is a symbol of defiance! On top of that, it is not one snake but two! When you start looking, it is interesting how many things you begin to see where Satan has infiltrated society with his perverted lies and arrogance against God and His people.

Satan hijacked and has perverted the rainbow—a promise of God—and he will try to hijack your authority that stands against him. He must break that **chain of authority**. He wants to stop that power from flowing into his domain. How does he do that? Through people of course. And like the snakes on that pole, it is easy to assume that you know what is going on. But you need to take a second look and trust the Holy Spirit to help you sniff out Satan's plans before they manifest. There are many tactics he will use, more than I could cover here, but let me name a few of the most common strategies he uses to sneak into your occupation team.

The number one way Satan gains access to your authority is through ignorance. So many believers are still praying to God to fix their problems. "God, you do something about it. You do something about this sickness. You do something about this poverty. You do something about...." They don't realize that He's already given them the authority to deal with it. This is why I have spent so much time helping you understand the authority you have in Christ in the first part of this book.

> **THE NUMBER ONE WAY SATAN GAINS ACCESS TO YOUR AUTHORITY IS THROUGH IGNORANCE.**

> *Truly I tell you, whatever you **bind** on earth will be bound in heaven, and whatever you loose on earth will be loosed in heaven.*
>
> —Matthew 18:18

So, what are you binding? What are you loosing? He's given you the keys to the Kingdom. You have that authority. Use the keys! But sadly, so many people, so many Christians still say things like "God allows bad things to happen. God kills people." Friend, we are talking about basic 101 Kingdom law here, even below 101. If they do not understand this basic fact of Kingdom life, how would they ever be able to rule over the enemy or carry their delegated authority? No, It's not possible. They will not be able to do it!

Consider it pure joy, my brothers and sisters, whenever you face trials of many kinds, because you know that the testing of your faith produces perseverance. Let perseverance finish its work so that you may be mature and complete, not lacking anything. If any of you lacks wisdom, you should ask God, who gives generously to all without finding fault, and it will be given to you. But when you ask, you must believe and not doubt, because the one who doubts is like a wave of the sea, blown and tossed by the wind. That person should not expect to receive anything from the Lord. Such a person is double-minded and unstable in all they do.

—James 1:2-8

I love this Scripture because it gives you a great guideline about who you need on your occupation team. Let me go through the three points.

1. *"Consider it pure joy, my brothers and sisters, whenever you face trials of many kinds, because you know that the testing of your faith produces perseverance. Let perseverance finish its work so that you may be mature and complete, not lacking anything."*

Okay, point number one: They should realize there will be trials in any position of authority. Depending on how high up the authority chain you are going to place them, the more experience they will need in dealing with Satan's tactics. No matter where they are on your occupation hierarchy organizational chart, they should have some experience with trials and using God's Word to stand their ground when challenged. In a trial, James says that a believer "KNOWS" that the testing of their faith cannot fail. Through perseverance, or not quitting and staying steadfast on the Word, they will be complete and lacking—NOTHING! The Word never fails. You do not want an immature believer calling you crying and wringing their hands in fear asking how to deal with every little problem that comes along. You want someone who can hold their position in agreement with the Word and with the assignment given to them.

> 2. *"If any of you lacks wisdom, you should ask God, who gives generously to all without finding fault, and it will be given to you."*

They know that they can go to God for wisdom in how to handle the trials they find themselves in and He will give it liberally.

> 3. *"But when you ask, you must believe and not doubt, because the one who doubts is like a wave of the sea, blown and tossed by the wind. That person should not expect to receive anything from the Lord. Such a person is double-minded and unstable in all they do."*

Lastly, they know they are not double-minded, so they EXPECT everything they need from the Lord!

In contrast, if you put a weak person in a position, one who is weak in faith and untested, this Scripture says they will be unstable in ALL their ways—ALL their ways. If you have a business, are you going to put some employee on the front line who is unstable?

If you were commanding an army, would you give an

assignment, a vital assignment where many lives matter, to someone you know is unstable? Someone who does not know how to handle his sword? No, you would not.

Unfortunately, it seems so many Christians are just learning how to keep the devil out of their own houses. Until they learn how to do that, please do not give them more responsibility. You cannot have wishy-washy people on your team and expect to win. Know what the Word says, and then stand on it. Well, Gary, I'm still afraid. Well, that's fine. Everyone grows up and learns who they are, but you need to win that battle at home before you can handle a public battle.

YOU CANNOT HAVE WISHY-WASHY PEOPLE ON YOUR TEAM AND EXPECT TO WIN.

Goliath was not David's first day out. When no one knew David's name and he was a shepherd for his father, he actually took on a bear and a lion with his bare hands as they threatened the family's sheep. That is some pretty intense stuff! So, David was not immune to hard times. Even though his life was worth much more than the sheep he was guarding, he was faithful to the trust given to him. Goliath was just another situation to David. What he had done in private with no one watching, he then did in the public arena. He had already been trained and tested to handle it. God knew the training David had to go through to be able to occupy his destiny.

Or take Joseph, for another example. He was sold into slavery by his brothers and ended up in Egypt, in Potiphar's house as a slave. But it just so happened that Potiphar was the captain of the palace guard. Coincidence? Not at all. It was there that Joseph learned proper Egyptian protocol and how Egyptian politics worked. He also got to see how Pharoah ruled, and he learned the laws of Egypt. Being a Hebrew, he had no experience in that area, but his destiny demanded that he know it.

Secondly, he was thrown into prison, which seemed like a horrible misfortune. But this was the doorway to meet two of Pharaoh's royal staff members who had been thrown into prison. One was eventually released to his former duties alongside Pharoah and when released would remember that Joseph had interpreted a dream showing that he would indeed be placed back in the royal court.

Finally, when Pharaoh himself had a dream that no one could interpret, the staff member who had been in prison told Pharoah about the man in prison who could interpret dreams. Pharoah called for Joseph, who successfully interpreted his dream. Through Joseph's journey, he learned everything he needed to know about the nation and administration, so the day he stood before Pharoah, he did not appear empty-handed. He also carried with him a plan of administration for the nation of Egypt to survive the coming famine. Pharoah was so impressed that he took his ring off his finger and placed it on Joseph's. Joseph was placed as second to Pharoah to rule over all of the land of Egypt.

Throughout the entire journey, Joseph stayed faithful, did whatever he was asked to do with excellence, and never wavered in his confidence that God would one day bring him out of that prison.

You see, Joseph is best remembered for interpreting Pharoah's dream, but the dream was not Joseph's greatest moment. His greatest moment was when he was standing before Pharoah with the plan of administration that would save Egypt as well as his own family from starvation. You see, the dream and interpretation were to give him credibility and were the means to give him an audience before Pharoah.

I always ask, "What will you say when you stand before Pharoah?" What will you say when you stand at the crossroads of the opportunity of a lifetime? If you have been faithful and diligent on your journey, you will stand before that moment of decision with confidence and the ability to say, "Yes."

God's not going to send you on an assignment to occupy territory on behalf of His Kingdom when you're unstable, wavering back and forth, and untrained. Well, can I trust God in this situation? If you have to ask that question, then the answer would be, "No." If you find that you are afraid, you had better stay put. But, Gary, I don't like my job. You're staying put. In fact, the more you don't like your job, the better. You're learning submission with a good heart, and you're learning to do things as unto the Lord. Until you persevere as unto the Lord, He can't trust you. You must win the private battle before God will put you in the public battle. Amen.

> **GOD'S NOT GOING TO SEND YOU ON AN ASSIGNMENT TO OCCUPY TERRITORY ON BEHALF OF HIS KINGDOM WHEN YOU'RE UNSTABLE, WAVERING BACK AND FORTH, AND UNTRAINED.**

God is protecting not only you, but He's also protecting His name.

Whoever can be trusted with very little can also be trusted with much, and whoever is dishonest with very little will also be dishonest with much. So if you have not been trustworthy in handling worldly wealth, who will trust you with true

riches? And if you have not been trustworthy with someone else's property, who will give you property of your own?
—Luke 16:10-12

You're in training. You're going to start out in training. But, Gary, I don't like my boss. You've got to change your mindset. If you want to be effective, you must be trained. Can the boss trust you with his company, with his money? If you understand that you have been given trust with someone else's property at that job, you will realize that your next promotion will be based on how well you do with that responsibility. Your assignment while you are there is not about you but about your boss, the one who hired you. Can your boss trust you to accomplish what he has assigned you to do?

But, Gary, I really don't like my boss. That's beside the point. Do you think that Joseph liked being a slave to Potiphar? Do you think that Joseph like being in that prison? Yet he did such a great job that the jailer put him in charge of the entire prison. The Lord is the one who promotes you. He knew where Joseph was in prison. He knew where Moses was out in the wilderness. He knew where David was with the sheep. He knows your name. Don't you think He knows your name? He knows your name. He knows where you're at.

I remember when we had just started television. It was a huge undertaking. Yes, I was scared. I really did not want to do it. The money it cost was in the millions and was hard for me grasp. But early on, when we had just stepped out on a local network, my secretary called me and said that a lady had just called in and, in tears, ordered everything we had. Every product we had, she bought. She went on to tell my secretary that she and her husband were facing some challenging situations. She said that she had a dream the night before where she saw me and heard my name. She said that this puzzled her as she did not know who I was or anything about me. She woke her husband and asked him if he knew a Gary Keesee, and he said no. The next morning, she turned on the TV and was shocked to see me there on her screen talking about how to get out of debt. She then called and told my secretary to send her everything we had.

Do you know how that encouraged me? I was facing a hard time, but I was faithful to push through it. And God took the time to remind me that He knew my name. Wow—that was great! So be of good courage; He knows your name too. The hard times you may be facing are helping you learn to be faithful. So, whatever you are doing, if you love it or not, do it with your whole heart as unto the Lord, and He will reward you. Secondly, look for people who have taken the same road of faithfulness that you have taken, and you will find your occupation team!

In our discussion, we indicated that ignorance is a major doorway that Satan uses to gain access to your team. Secondly, we want to talk about a mistake that every leader makes putting immature people in a place of authority before they are ready.

> *Brothers, I could not address you as spiritual, but as worldly—mere infants in Christ.*
>
> —1 Corinthians 3:1 (BSB)

If you are leading people, you need to realize that Satan will send people, and God will send people. If you have a business, Satan will send people. If you have a church, Satan will send people. And then people will also send themselves your way, desiring to be on your team. And they all may look very talented. And they're almost always very flattering. But I have learned the hard way. I don't care what they say or what their credentials are. They ALL need to be tested first, before you put them into a position. Get some tissues ready as I share some of my worst stories of violating this essential principle.

> **IF YOU ARE LEADING PEOPLE, YOU NEED TO REALIZE THAT SATAN WILL SEND PEOPLE, AND GOD WILL SEND PEOPLE.**

PEOPLE, YOUR ANSWER OR YOUR PROBLEM: PART TWO

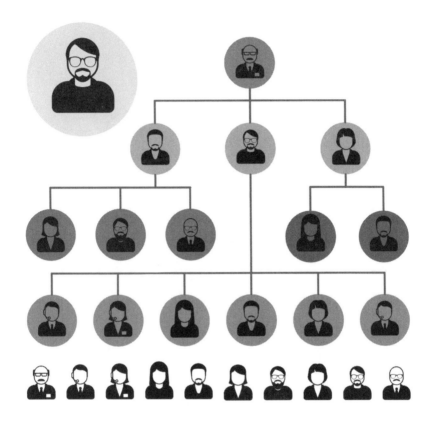

Take a good look at the above picture, because you will need to draw one just like it to be able to occupy the territory that God calls you to. As you can see in this picture, every part, each person in every box, must be faithful to their authority and the fulfillment of their designated assignment for their box. Paul uses an example of the human body to illustrate that every part needs to function for the body to grow.

> From him the whole body, joined and held together by **every** supporting ligament, grows and builds itself up in love, as each **part** does its work.

> —Ephesians 4:16

Every part working with its unique function provides the complete picture of the King's will, the authority of the Kingdom flowing down into the earth realm.

You're in one of those boxes, or possibly several, and you're part of that puzzle, that complete picture. If the person in one of the boxes fails to perform, tries to change the objective, or is unclear what the king's will is, we have a problem. The entire structure becomes dysfunctional, a dysfunctional organization that is not in alignment with the head. It becomes a dysfunctional org. chart. To be dysfunctional means it's not functioning. It's useless as far as bringing the will of the king or CEO into reality. It cannot accomplish or finish that task.

> EVERY PART WORKING WITH ITS UNIQUE FUNCTION PROVIDES THE COMPLETE PICTURE OF THE KING'S WILL, THE AUTHORITY OF THE KINGDOM FLOWING DOWN INTO THE EARTH REALM.

Now, the point I have made in this entire book is that each person must be in their assigned place. To be in alignment with the king, you must be in alignment with the one you report to. I did not say you have to like them. I said you had to be in alignment with the instructions they are getting from their leader. There is no other option, no other play here. The success of the entire organization depends on it. This is why the first thing they teach you in the military is to obey orders.

Ignorance is the basic beginning point of failure, as we have seen. If you don't understand your personal authority, am I going to put you in a place of authority? No. Neither is God. This is why the enemy has tried to convince most of the churches that God does bad things to good people. If you cannot trust Him, you will not follow His direction and will question His motives.

But if people understand that God is good and only good, and His promises mean exactly what they say, then people will line up behind that. God's power will flow and become dangerous to the enemy.

Let me paraphrase what I just said so it applies to the secular realm. If you do not know how your company structure works, where you're at on that org. chart, you need to find out. If you are all over the place, talking to anyone and everyone about what you think about everything that does not pertain to your area of responsibility, talking about how you do not agree with the direction that the company is taking, then you become a dysfunctional, dangerous person on that org. chart and to the company. You may think, *Well, I only talk to people when the boss is not around.* But you know what? God sees all of it.

Everyone wants promotion, but so many do not pay the price to be qualified. Let me illustrate with a story. It's the story of Saul, the first king of Israel. The prophet, Samuel, had anointed him as king, but then there was a problem. God told Samuel to go to Saul and tell him he had been disqualified and could no longer be the king. I think your next questions should be, "Why? How did King Saul become disqualified?" Well, the Amalekites were attacking Israel and had set themselves against the Lord. So, God told King Saul to wipe them out. Saul was also instructed to not bring any of the animals back with them. Beginning in 1 Samuel 15:13, we see Saul speaking to Samuel after returning from the battle.

EVERYONE WANTS PROMOTION, BUT SO MANY DO NOT PAY THE PRICE TO BE QUALIFIED.

> *"I have carried out the Lord's instructions."*
>
> *But Samuel said, "What then is this bleating of sheep in my ears? What is this lowing of cattle?"*
>
> *Saul answered, "The soldiers brought them ... they spared the best of the sheep and cattle to sacrifice to the Lord your God, but we totally destroyed the rest."*
>
> —1 Samuel 15:13b-15

And Samuel said, "Enough!" I think what he meant was, "I don't want to hear your excuses. I don't want to hear your better idea. I don't want to hear your thoughts of how it should have been done. I'm not interested in hearing that."

Samuel said, "The Lord talked to me about you last night." "Well, tell me," Saul said.

> *Samuel said, "Although you were once small in your own eyes, did you not become the head of the tribes of Israel? The Lord anointed you king over Israel. And he sent you on a mission saying, 'Go and completely destroy those wicked people, the Amalekites. Wage war against them until you have wiped them out.' Why did you not obey the Lord? Why did you pounce on the plunder and do evil in the eyes of God?"*
>
> —1 Samuel 15:17-18

<u>Verse 20 gives him away. What were his first words?</u> **"But I *did* obey."** Whoa, back up. Samuel repeated exactly what God had said to King Saul, and, again, Saul countered it with, "But I did obey." Yet he did not do what God said, did he?

To make a long story short, he disqualified himself. God said,

"Can't have this." If you want to be qualified for promotion in life, you need to do what those in authority over you ask you to do. Pretty simple, isn't it?

Your kids say, "I cleaned my room." So, you want to go and check it out, to verify that it is indeed cleaned. So, you go into their bedroom, and it looks great until you look under the bed. They just threw everything under the bed, right? Threw everything in the closet. No, no, no, no. Nice try, but no, no. We need to show you how to really do this. When you're 50 years old and still throwing stuff under the bed, we have a problem, because God can't trust you. And when you're 50 years old, it won't simply be clothes under the bed. It might be not claiming all your income on your tax return or cheating on your wife if you don't get this straightened out.

> *Whoever walks in integrity walks securely, but whoever takes crooked paths will be found out.*
> —Proverbs 10:9

We live in an instant society where everyone is promoting themselves and trying to bypass God's promotion system. I was never more shocked than when I saw two young people from our youth department advertising themselves as life coaches. Really! I see all the glamour shots the young ladies are putting on Instagram. Everyone wants to be famous, a movie star. In reality, self-promotion does not work. Because even though a person may look perfect on their social media account, when you hire them, you may find that they do not have a clue. And secondly, you do not want to get ahead of your character and your wisdom and promote yourself into a disaster.

We were a young church, with maybe 70 people attending, when our drummer called in sick for Wednesday night service. I had this brilliant idea, as a young pastor that knew no better, to ask if anyone there played the drums. A young man stepped up and said he did. I asked him if he was a good drummer, and he said yes. I never really knew that he was a drummer, but he had been attending the church for a while, so I said to go ahead. Well, you can imagine what happened. He could not hold a beat if his life depended on it. It got so bad that we had to stop him and have him sit down. Then, of course, he felt humiliated, which was not my intention, but he left me no choice. Well, let me back up. He did give me a choice. I was the immature pastor that brought him up there.

Or take the time that one of my elders came to my office before service and told me one of the greeters who manned the front door was passing out an invitation to everyone who came through to a picnic she was hosting the following Sunday starting at the exact time that our service started. I could not believe it! I had to correct that situation in a hurry from the podium. People that have not been taught or tested should never be put in a position of authority, even if it is something as simple as being a greeter! As a leader, you do not want to be surprised by someone's incompetence or their bad attitude after the fact. Without exception, let a man be tested before you place them in a position of authority. Every business owner has found out that the resume doesn't quite tell you the whole story.

> **PEOPLE THAT HAVE NOT BEEN TAUGHT OR TESTED SHOULD NEVER BE PUT IN A POSITION OF AUTHORITY.**

I've had people on staff through the years that had side ministries or side businesses. Now, I am all for doing things on the side. I usually encourage it as long as they fulfill their obligation to me with excellence. But on more than one occasion, I would find my staff member hanging around our guest speakers with their brochures in hand, talking to them about using their side hustle company for this or that. I am always shocked at people's lack of common sense and lack of integrity. More than once, I found my vendors had hired out my staff after hours to work on their projects while my projects were late.

So many people are hirelings. They are with you as long as there are no better offers somewhere else. You can't trust people that promote themselves to carry out your instructions. Over the years, I have had employees that work in the computer department, let's say. And it was like pulling teeth to get things done well and on time. But I would go online to their Facebook pages or their websites, because they had these little side businesses, something they were doing. And I have been so shocked to find their websites laid out so perfectly, and so vibrant, with illustrations and pictures. And every link **worked**! (I think all leaders know why I bolded and underlined **worked**.) If I go down through their pages, I am impressed with the excellence they are portraying, but many times, I find no mention of any event at church, ever. How can you work full-time somewhere as exciting as a church without saying anything about the men's meeting or the breakfast or the VBS?

That kind of tells you where they are at, right?

People who promote themselves will always choose themselves in a decision. They will always choose themselves in a decision, because they'll always put themselves first. They're always subconsciously looking for a better-paying job; they look at everyplace they work as a stepping stone to their next opportunity. Now, if you asked them if that was true, they'd say no. But subconsciously, they're always looking. They're always open. They're always kind of, "this is temporary" in their mindset. You might say, "Well, Pastor Gary, what's wrong with that?" Well, I don't believe the church operates like the world does.

> **PEOPLE WHO PROMOTE THEMSELVES WILL ALWAYS CHOOSE THEMSELVES IN A DECISION.**

Here's what I mean by that. When God called Drenda and me to launch Faith Life Church, we didn't have a list of options if it didn't work out. God said, "Launch a church." We knew it was going to cost us something. We did not launch the church to make money. We launched the church because God said to do it. We covered much of the expenses, paid a lot of the payroll, and emptied our bank accounts more than once. We did not take a salary for years after the church started but instead earned our own money from our business.

Now, I believe my staff members should feel called here. I do not mean they need to come here thinking they will be here forever, but they need to know that God has led them here. If God tells you that you're to be someplace, you can put your resume away because you know you are where you are supposed to be. God will tell you when it's time to investigate another option. But if you come in on day one and search Google for a better job that same night, we have a problem. Now, there are positions in every organization that are designed to be temporary. I am not talking about those types of positions. Listen, God knows where you are at; He knows your name. You don't have to be second-guessing every move you make.

Slaves [employees], obey your earthly masters with respect and fear and with sincerity of heart, just as you would obey Christ. Obey them not only to win their favor when their eye is on you, but as slaves of Christ, doing the will of God from your heart. Serve wholeheartedly, as if you were serving the Lord, not people, because you know the Lord will reward each one for whatever good they do, whether they are slave or free.

—Ephesians 6:5-8

Joseph didn't market himself on Facebook out of prison, right? God brought him out, and God will move you too. He knows the plans He has for you more than you even want great plans for yourself. He knows exactly what you're being mentored for.

You do not know what you don't know. God knows where you're headed, and that place you may despise working at now is part of your mentoring needed to be somewhere else someday. "But Gary, I already told you I hate my job." "That's good." That means you must choose to submit, not that you want to submit. You need that. You need to choose to submit, because that is how authority operates.

Yet, you'll not be there that long. If you submit to that job with a willing heart and you're the best on the team, guaranteed, God will move you on. He'll show you the next step. Now, if you want to stay there forever, just keep mumbling and complaining how you hate going to work and all that, and you'll be there a while or at a different place like that one.

When I went to college and came out with an Old Testament major, God did not tell me what I would be doing. I wasn't called to pastor then. He just said, "You're going to preach My Word."

When I got out of school, I thought, *What's next?* Well, as I told you before, He led me into finances. I was shocked! Into finances! I knew I was called to preach; what was going on? Let me tell you how He led me, and I think it will serve as an example of how we allow God to move us into our destiny and why we must be faithful to wherever He leads us.

When I was in college, I worked for a window blind company, installing draperies and mini blinds. As you already know, I did not do that well in high school, especially in Math. But one day as I was working in the back room at the blind company, my boss's insurance man came in, sat down in his office, and began to talk to him about insurance. Because I was in the next room, I could hear what they were saying. Strangely, I was mesmerized by the conversation. I remember thinking how interesting all that was. A few weeks later, I received a call from a guy who was hiring people to work in the financial field selling life insurance. He invited me down to his office, and after seeing all that he was doing, again, something in me wanted to join. But I was confused. God had called me to preach when I was 19. What about that?

Well, to make a long story short, I took the job, and, as I previously said in the book, I had to make cold calls and was on straight commissions, which I hated! So, I quit and hired on at a landscape company for a while, actually two weeks. I found out very quickly that digging ditches in the 103-degree heat was not for me. So, I went back to selling insurance. But, oh, how I wanted a good job instead of all that calling. I would drive home at night after being on those calls all-day long in the office, go home for supper, then get ready to go on appointments at night. I'd pass these guys getting home in their yards, just spending time with their families. I thought, "If I could have a job where you just punch a clock and you leave it behind then retire broke, that'd be great."

Oh, no. God had a plan. But I had to walk it out. As I said, eventually, I got better at what I did, and we became the number one office out of 5,000 offices in the U.S. for one of our key vendors. At one point, I had 300 reps nationwide—all working for me. I learned a lot. I needed to learn a lot to be able to pastor God's people. God knew where I was headed, but I didn't.

When you come under someone else's authority, you lose some of your freedom; many things are not your choice anymore.

JUST STAY WHERE YOU ARE AT UNTIL GOD SAYS TO MOVE. BE LOYAL AND OBEDIENT TO THE AUTHORITY THAT GOD HAS PUT YOU UNDER.

But you really do not need to know too much at that point. Just stay where you are at until God says to move. Be loyal and obedient to the authority that God has put you under.

I tell my staff in their employee handbook they are not to be seen at an R-rated movie in a movie theater. They're not to be seen there. Well, why is that, Pastor? I mean, I'm not at work. Yes, you are, because you represent me and this church wherever you go. If people see you at an R-rated movie, they will think, *Well, Pastor Gary must go to R-rated movies. It must be okay with him.* Let this sink in. When they see you, they see your boss, whoever that might be. The members of my church staff represent me when they are out in public. The members of my business team at Forward Financial Group represent me. I am not free to just do whatever I want to do.

When my people go to the hospital to pray for people, I tell them they must not dishonor me. If they go into the hospital and say, "Pastor Gary's been out of town all week, and he's not here. I thought I'd come by and pray with you. He couldn't be here." What does that sound like? "Pastor Gary's too busy for you or he doesn't care for you. That's why I didn't show up, right? Pastor Gary doesn't care for you. He's traveling around doing his thing, whatever. Here you are in the hospital. He's flying around, just.... What does that sound like? Pastor Gary doesn't care for you, but I do. That is totally wrong because, first off, they wouldn't be in the position unless I brought them into the position. I laid my hands on them. They have my anointing, and they represent me when they go there. You represent your CEO wherever you're at. You are representing the authorities over you.

Anyway, Paul talked about self-promotion in 1 Corinthians 3. Remember, we talked about that in a previous chapter. That church in Corinth was all about self-promotion, because they were babies.

These are baby Christians. Babies cannot be promoted into a place of authority. Babies think they're mature when they're babies. Babies think because they have giftings by the Holy Spirit, they're mature enough to walk into a place of responsibility.

> YOU NEED TO BE MENTORED, AND GROW, AND MATURE FROM BEING A BABY TO A PERSON THAT CAN HANDLE RESPONSIBILITY AND AUTHORITY.

You or someone you know have kids that want to drive at age nine? They're not ready for that. You need to be mentored, and grow, and mature from being a baby to a person that can handle responsibility and authority.

Now, remember James 3:16? We read from that previously in

this book as well. *"Where you have envy and selfish ambition, there you'll find"*—what? Everyone out of order and the org. chart a big, fighting mess—*"disorder and every evil practice."* In fact, some versions say, "There's confusion and every evil work." There's no flow of authority. Everyone's out for themselves. Everyone thinks they have a better idea. Everyone thinks they should be boss. Kind of sounds like the country, doesn't it? Kind of. Anyway, things become a big mess. Nothing good comes out of disorder. You will not be able to occupy anything in that mess. God's power can't flow down through that mess.

I remember talking to a pastor who had a large church. He said he was having all kinds of problems. So, he brought in a new COO to help him. I was with that COO when I talked to this pastor. The first thing he did was to fire about one-third of the staff and redesign the org. chart. He looked for people that wanted to be there, that went the extra mile and smiled while they did.

ANOTHER AREA WHERE THE ENEMY COMES IN TO STEAL YOUR FUTURE, TO GET YOU OUT OF ORDER, IS BY LURING YOU INTO TAKING FALSE RESPONSIBILITY.

Well, that pastor's church took off. In five years, it grew to six times the size it had been and became a worldwide ministry.

You need to deal with the chaos and put order into your org. chart. Remember, babies are all about me, me, me. That is okay when they are young in the Lord and they are growing. But you certainly would never put a baby in a place of authority. They usually do not even know what authority is at that point. They just want their milk and to be put to bed.

Another area where the enemy comes in to steal your future, to get you out of order, is by luring you into taking false responsibility. False responsibility is trying to fix something without having the authority to fix it. Have you ever done that? It cost you a lot of money, didn't it? Yeah. Taking on someone else's responsibility... I have endless stories like that, and I've done it myself. I think we've all done that.

I remember one family, years ago, they were losing their house, and they told everyone about it. Now typically, you would think that people would not want to share that they were losing their house. In church, that's a good place to do it, because someone may want to help you out. I'm not against generosity. Please understand me.

The problem was this person didn't have a job. I talked to him about that. I said, "Why don't you have a job? Your house is going into foreclosure." "Well, I'm waiting for this other job to open up." I said, "Well, you can get a job while you are waiting for that dream job to open someday. I'll even help you find...." "No, no, I don't want those jobs. I'm believing for this certain job."

I was thinking, *Are you kidding me? You're going to let your family starve and lose your house? There is provision on the way to your promise. I mean, come on. You've got to feed the family while you're looking and waiting for that job.* A family in the church gave him the $10,000, and he got the house caught up, but they lost the house in three months anyway. It was foreclosed on.

What happened? I will tell you what happened. Their training had been delayed by three months, by good intentions, but nevertheless, it short-circuited their training for three months and cost their friends $10,000.

Well, Pastor, aren't we to be generous? Yes, but it has to be met with responsibility. When people come to Faith Life and say, "Hey, I can't pay my bills," we have a plan and a process to help them. We don't take on the responsibility of paying their bills. We'll help them one month and maybe two at the most, but during that time, we put them in a training system of financial management.

We work with them, help them get stable, but we do not pay their bills. You have to meet us halfway. You've got to do your part. We're not the piggy bank. You are the one who is responsible for the issues, and you will have to admit that and take ownership. God will help you.

As I said previously, I meet so many grandmas that are broke because they're paying all their kids' bills. Stop it, Grandma. Stop it. Well, they'll starve to death. Well, I guarantee they won't starve to death. They may starve a little bit, but that's a good starve. If they get hungry enough, they will work it out. Taking false responsibility for someone else does not allow them to grow up.

When we started our church, I had never seen an org. chart because I was in sales. I had reps and maybe three secretaries, but they were all self-governed. My sales reps were all on commissions, meaning that if they didn't work, they didn't eat. I would help license them, train them, and motivate them, but they had to take responsibility for their own income, because it was based on commissions.

I never hired people as employees until we started the church. As it grew, I knew I needed some help, so I hired a few employees. But I found out very quickly that managing sales reps and managing employees were two different things altogether. Well, we would have weekly staff meetings, and here is how they usually went.

"Pastor, we have a big church picnic coming up, as you know. Do you want hot dogs or hamburgers? Oh, should we provide ketchup, mustard? How about mayonnaise? What do you want there? Paper plates or plastic plates? What color do you want them to be? Do you want us to email that information out to the church, or do you want to announce it from the podium? How about hot chocolate? Should we have that?"

Now, you multiply those questions times five, seven, ten employees, it will drive you nuts. But I didn't know any better; it was all new to me. No one ever taught me how this works. I thought it was my responsibility to have all the answers and to make all the decisions. You can guess what happened. I began to despise my position. I was micromanaged into complete dysfunction. I told Drenda one day, "I'm resigning. I love my company, and I love God, but I don't like pastoring a church. It's just not working."

We had a pastor come through the church as a guest speaker, and we were talking with him about all the dysfunction we were dealing with. Then he said something that totally changed my perspective of things. He said, "Gary, you don't owe your church the responsibility of fixing all their personal problems. All you owe them is to be an example and to have fun.'

I understood the example part. I had the example. My marriage was great, we were out of debt, and we had seen God do mighty things. So, I understood being an example. I felt that our family was a great example of the reality of God's Kingdom. I understood that. But did he say fun? That kind of threw me. I said, "You said fun, didn't you?" He said, "Yes." Fun. Are you kidding? Fun?

I mean, I had everyone's problem. I was thinking about everyone's problem. I was taking false responsibility for their marriages, for their bills. I was thinking of their kids. I was thinking of all this stuff, right? I told him that I wouldn't wish this chaos on my worst enemy, let alone be an inspiration to others that want to follow into the ministry.

Friend, that's not how it works. I had no idea how to occupy for God. But I have a great wife who wanted to help me find out how. Drenda found a gentleman who helps pastors and leaders learn how to lead, how to occupy for God. His name is Dean Radtke, and he works with leaders all over the world.

We located a conference he was speaking at, and we went. When I met Dean Radtke, he talked about all the pastors and leaders that are quitting every day because Bible schools don't teach you how to pastor, with administration, and legal issues, and HR departments, and health insurance, and tax issues, all that stuff. They don't teach you that. The same goes for business owners who have a great idea and jump out into it and start drowning in the details.

At his conference, he had three big whiteboards up front, and he filled up every one of them. I was like, "Okay. This is really intense here." I really did not understand half of what he was saying, but I knew beneath all the data was the answer I needed.

Drenda lined it up for me and her to sit down with Dean for three days, nonstop from 9:00 a.m. till 10:00 p.m. Yes, those were three intense days. He just very slowly went through all those charts, over and over.

One thing caught my attention. He said, "Gary, it's going to get worse. You will need to get better." That's when I thought, *I'm almost done with you*, but he was right. You must get better. You must learn how that authority flows, who's responsible.

He said, "Stay in the box." He pointed to that org. chart he had drawn on the big whiteboard and said, "Gary, you've got to stay in the box. You're the leader. You don't want to jump down here four layers deep and help them stuff boxes for the weekend service. You're the head. You give instruction and direction."

In fact, here's what he said my job was. This is the job of anyone who is leading a team of people. You provide direction and expectation. You obtain plans, ideas, and recommendations from your team. Then, you approve a plan and commission the work. You provide the tools necessary to ensure success. Then you obtain evaluation to further tweak the plan later.

I remember thinking, *Wow, that's different.* That was the first time I learned about a chart with boxes that shows you how authority flows in a government, church, or business. It's called government. It's called learning how authority flows. He said, "Stay in the box. If your name's in the box, you have it. If your name's in the box, you're responsible." You don't need to be hopping over to someone else's box. You have your box, and you're responsible for it. To be effective, you need to know what box you are reporting to above you on the chart and what boxes are under your responsibility, who is reporting to you. That is all you really need to focus on.

It was so important to learn that. If you understand an org. chart and have been trained in corporate America, you are probably laughing, but seriously, I had no idea. Here is the mistake I was making. I was hiring people who needed help instead of hiring people that could help me. I was hiring people who did not know much more than I did instead of people who knew a lot of things I did not know that I needed to know. I needed people with strengths and knowledge that I didn't have. It was definitely a change for me, but learning how an org. chart works completely changed my life. Our ministry grew to become a worldwide ministry in more than 60 nations and on daily TV in every time zone in the world. Thousands of people have had their lives changed because Drenda and I, just two people, did not quit. Yes, Dean Radtke was right: It was going to get worse, and I had to get better. He was so right. I just needed a little coaching on how the org. chart works, how authority flows down through the boxes with precision and accountability.

Another way Satan likes to disrupt the flow of authority is through what I call hijacking authority. Let's go back to our story regarding King Saul being disqualified. After Saul was set down, God then had to find a new king. The prophet Samuel was instructed to go to the house of a man named Jesse. He was told that once there, God would show him who the new king was. Samuel arrived at Jesse's house and said, "Get all your sons up here; line them up. The Holy Spirit is going to tell me who the next king is."

ANOTHER WAY SATAN LIKES TO DISRUPT THE FLOW OF AUTHORITY IS THROUGH WHAT I CALL HIJACKING AUTHORITY.

The sons began to assemble, and in walked Eliab, tall and handsome. Samuel thought to himself, *That's him. That's the guy.* But God said to him, "That is not the guy." Why? Because God looks at the inward heart, but men look at the outward appearance.

This is a mistake we all make. I call it being hijacked by talent, moved by flattery, or moved by appearance. We put people in places where they are not mature enough to be in that position. I think if you own any company or pastor a church, you have probably made that mistake and you know what I'm talking about when

I say hijacked by talent.

They're so good at what they do. I mean, I know there are some issues with their character, but how would I find anyone that can do what they do? They're talented. Do you understand what I'm talking about? You delay confronting them, and you walk on eggshells to keep them. You even raise their pay to appease them, but you already know they are not with you. You already know that if you had someone else just as talented, you would set them down. But you don't, so you put up with it. You continue to compromise.

Dean Radtke said, "You would have a better worship service with only a juice harp and someone who knew they were not the best, but truly wanted to worship and be part of your team, than with a team of worship leaders whose hearts are whacked out with pride." Dean told me, "Gary, you've got to clear the air. You've got to confront this situation and deal with it. You can't be insecure in leadership. You don't judge people by their talent or by their resume. You've got to get in there and do what God is telling you. I know he looks great, has awesome talent, but God is saying, "That's not the guy." Here comes the devil's blackmail statement: "You do not have anyone to take their place!" But I know someone who does. God already knew of a young man who had His heart, a young man who was a nobody out tending sheep for his dad. His name was David, the next king of Israel.

When God spoke to me in Albania that I was to launch a TV ministry, that was something I had never thought of and never wanted to think of. I knew nothing about doing TV. But in Albania, God told me He was sending me to the nations, and TV was the means by which He was going to do it. But there were some major hurdles to overcome before that could happen. First, it would cost about $300,000 to get things started. Secondly, as I said, I did not know anything about doing TV. I had no equipment and no people on staff that knew anything about TV. The church was in the middle of building the Now Center campus, and every cent was already allocated toward that project. There was no money. In my mind, it was an impossible mandate. I just could not see how it could happen. I wrestled with that decision for a month. I was miserable! Finally, I said, "Yes." I did not know how, but I said yes.

In a Sunday morning service, a man in my church, who came to my church about two years earlier broke, walked up to me and gave me $120,000 toward TV. I was totally shocked. Then through some other events that God arranged, Drenda and I had the $300,000. Wow!

Then an even more amazing event happened. Drenda was at a meeting, and a lady that she did not know said to her, "If you guys ever do TV, call this guy." Drenda had not mentioned anything to her about doing TV; she had just met her. The lady wrote down the man's name and email address, and Drenda stuck it in her purse.

A couple of weeks later, Drenda remembered the note she received from the lady and decided to email the man. He answered and said he would like to meet us. We made arrangements to meet, and at the meeting, we explained how God had spoken to us about doing TV. It was a great meeting, and we left him with some of our material. He said that he would call us back. Eventually, he called us back and said that he would help us with our TV program. On top of that, he said that he would provide all the equipment as well as edit and produce the show. We were thrilled and set up a time to meet at our home to design a place in our home where we could tape the programs. That day arrived, and for the first time, he shared with us his history of producing TV. He told us how he was working with almost every major ministry on TV at that time. I sat there stunned. I remember thinking, *How did this guy, someone with his experience, end up in my house out in the country on my dirt road?*" Only God could do that.

In another situation, Drenda was told through a dream to support a ministry couple that we had known for a while, and we were to become major supporters of what they were doing. Their ministry is known for sending teaching materials all over the world. Well, since God had spoken to me about going to the nations, that fit my passion perfectly. We love supporting them, and we are and have been supporting them for years.

But one day, God spoke to me that He wanted me to translate Drenda's and my Kingdom teachings and books into the world's languages and send them out. Well, I had been watching our friends do this for years. They have connections all over the world that can translate and print books and material. When I told my friends about what God said to me, they offered their translation and printing team to help. Now, we have translated our material into more than 50 different languages and counting and have small groups in more than 60 nations worldwide. The point being that God knew what we were to occupy when He told us to support that couple. That one connection was the key that enabled us to occupy the territory God had for us.

God knows where the people are. He will bring them, so don't allow yourself to be highjacked by someone's talent or charisma. God knows where the Davids are at, the graphics person you need or the IT person. He has been training them somewhere just for this moment, and He will speak to them!

Another tactic that Satan uses to gain access into your org. chart and wreak havoc is through an offense. This is a big one in the church. The enemy can launch offenses everywhere, right? We read what Paul said about that church in Corinth, that there was jealousy and quarreling. He said they were babies.

ANOTHER TACTIC THAT SATAN USES TO GAIN ACCESS INTO YOUR ORG. CHART AND WREAK HAVOC IS THROUGH AN OFFENSE.

Have you ever noticed how offended babies get? Wah. The baby picks up something you do not want them to have. No, no. Wah. They get all upset. My toy, my toy! Babies get offended so easily. They're going to get all upset because they didn't get to do this or that. You didn't give them the position or promotion they wanted, or you had to correct them. They will cry out, "That's not fair." You hear that a lot, "It's not fair." I think I have mentioned this before, but let's review:

NEVER PUT A BABY IN A PLACE OF AUTHORITY!

I'm not saying they can't grow up. I'm not trying to write people off. I want to write them in. But you will need to train and mentor these people, right? They all have giftings, and they all have assignments that God put in them to help you occupy the territory that God is calling you to occupy. As these offenses pop up, and they will, you will need to deal with them quickly before those involved go political with their offense and start recruiting people to their point of view. Soon, you will have a gang of people who have picked up the offense. Let's make one thing very clear. An offense stops the authority flowing down from the head quicker than a lightning bolt. You cannot let an offense fester. The Bible is clear on how to handle them.

> *If your brother or sister sins, go and point out their fault,*
> *just between the two of you. If they listen to you, you have won*
> *them over.*
>
> —Matthew 18:15

Go to that person. Don't go sideways. Don't gossip. Go to that person, right? If there is a problem that you can't handle, always go up with your comments, never sideways. In this type of situation, it is imperative that you keep the dialogue and the comments in proper alignment with the org. chart. I have found that most offenses are really just misunderstandings. Perceptions sometimes are greater than reality, and people like to read a lot of things that are not true into situations. If you have to, get the two offended parties together and talk it out. Usually, that will work things out.

As a leader, you are responsible for communicating with your team, the boxes under you on the org. chart. Good communication solves and prevents most of the problems people encounter and will keep the authority and the power of God flowing. Your occupation of the territory God has entrusted to you will be successful, and you will find promotion in your future.

Lastly, be diligent and serve the Lord with joy, and you will find that God will do amazing things in your life.

CHAPTER
EIGHT

MONEY IS NEEDED TO OCCUPY!

I do not think I have to mention the need for money. Money is required for anything in the earth realm. And if you are going to exercise your occupation over anything, it will require money. So, I wanted to spend at least one chapter on this topic, although I would encourage you to get my "Your Financial Revolution" book series to learn more.

I want you to think of a revolution. I am sure that you immediately thought of the French Revolution or the Civil War, where there was an attempt to overthrow an existing government and put a new government in place. This is exactly what Jesus did. He overthrew Satan's government, which had ruled over mankind for thousands of years. But Jesus stripped him of his power and ushered a new government into the earth realm—the Kingdom of God. As I stated in the beginning of this book, all kingdoms are governed by a king and a government, which carry his laws into every aspect of life in the kingdom.

IT IS THE LAWS OF THIS NEW KINGDOM, THE KINGDOM OF GOD, THAT CHANGED MY LIFE— AND IF YOU WILL TAKE THE TIME TO LEARN THOSE LAWS, THEY WILL CHANGE YOUR LIFE AS WELL.

When you were born again, you became a citizen of this great government, thus you have legal rights in God's Kingdom. However, so many Christians have not understood this fact and have never learned the laws that they have access to, especially in the area of finances. It is the laws of this new Kingdom, the Kingdom of God, that changed my life—and if you will take the time to learn those laws, they will change your life as well.

When Adam and Eve kicked God out of their lives, they came

under Satan's jurisdiction, his kingdom of sickness, poverty, and death. Satan became the god of this world. I did not say God; I said the god of this world.

> The **god of this age** has blinded the minds of unbelievers, so that they cannot see the light of the gospel that displays the glory of Christ, who is the image of God.
> —2 Corinthians 4:4

The Gospel of Luke gives us a good picture of what Satan took from Adam.

> The devil led him up to a high place and showed him in an instant all the kingdoms of the world. And he said to him, "I will give you all their authority and splendor; it has been given to me, and I can give it to anyone I want to. If you worship me, it will all be yours."
> —Luke 4:5-7

Wow, this shows us so much! The text says that Satan had obtained from Adam all the authority, which was the authority to rule over the earth with the spiritual position he had as a king. And secondly, Satan then had authority over the splendor of the kingdoms of the earth, the splendor being the wealth of the nations or kingdoms. But notice he said he could give it to anyone he chose to give it to. This is the tactic he uses today to lure people away from God.

But Jesus redeemed mankind, for all who would call upon Him, and returned to them the authority to rule over Satan, as we have been reading in the preceding chapters. By the power of the

Holy Spirit, we can prosper again. This deliverance out of Satan's poverty-stricken kingdom is called good news in Isaiah, where this complete deliverance from poverty was prophesied. I want to walk through this prophecy with you because it is talking about us, here in the church age, and describing a benefit that most of us, I am sure, would not want to miss. It is a lengthy prophetic word, but it is well worth taking the time to read.

> *The Spirit of the Sovereign Lord is on me, because the Lord has anointed me to* **_proclaim good news to the poor_***. He has sent me to bind up the brokenhearted, to proclaim freedom for the captives and release from darkness for the prisoners,* **_to proclaim the year of the Lord's favor_** *and the day of vengeance of our God, to comfort all who mourn, and provide for those who grieve in Zion—to bestow on them a crown of beauty instead of ashes, the oil of joy instead of mourning, and a garment of praise instead of a spirit of despair.*

> *They will be called oaks of righteousness,* **_a planting of the Lord for the display of his splendor_***. They will rebuild the ancient ruins and restore the places long devastated; they will renew the ruined cities that have been devastated for generations. Strangers will shepherd your flocks; foreigners will work your fields and vineyards.*

> *And you will be called priests of the Lord, you will be named ministers of our God. You will feed on the wealth of nations, and in their riches you will boast. Instead of your shame you will receive a double portion, and instead of disgrace you will rejoice in your inheritance. And so you will inherit a double portion in your land, and everlasting joy will be yours.*

> *"For I, the Lord, love justice; I hate robbery and wrong-*

doing. ___In my faithfulness I will reward my people and make___
___an everlasting covenant with them.___ *Their descendants will be*
known among the nations and their offspring among the peoples.
All who see them will acknowledge that they are a people
the Lord has blessed."

—Isaiah 61:1-9

First, before I cover a couple of vital facts about this prophecy,
I should mention that Jesus tells us in Luke 4 that He is the
fulfillment of this prophecy.

> *He went to Nazareth, where he had been brought up, and*
> *on the Sabbath day he went into the synagogue, as was his cus-*
> *tom. He stood up to read, and the scroll of the prophet Isaiah*
> *was handed to him. Unrolling it, he found the place where it*
> *is written:*
>
> > *"The Spirit of the Lord is on me, because he has*
> > *anointed me to proclaim good news to the poor. He has*
> > *sent me to proclaim freedom for the prisoners and re-*
> > *covery of sight for the blind, to set the oppressed free, to*
> > *proclaim the year of the Lord's favor."*
>
> *Then he rolled up the scroll, gave it back to the attendant*
> *and sat down. The eyes of everyone in the synagogue were*
> *fastened on him.* ___He began by saying to them, "Today this___
> ___scripture is fulfilled in your hearing.___*"*
>
> —Luke 4:16-21

Now that we know that the prophecy is speaking of the church age, we can easily assume that when the prophecy says this below that it is speaking of our new covenant through Jesus:

> ***In my faithfulness I will reward my people and make an everlasting covenant with them.*** *Their descendants will be known among the nations and their offspring among the peoples. All who see them will acknowledge that they are a people the Lord has blessed.*

Do you remember when the wise men came and brought gifts to Jesus when He was just a very small boy? We usually talk about the wise men coming to the manger at Christmas, but the Bible is clear that they did not come to the manger when Jesus was born but rather to his house later on.

> *On coming to the house, they saw the child with his mother Mary, and they bowed down and worshiped him. Then they opened their treasures and presented him with gifts of gold, frankincense and myrrh. And having been warned in a dream not to go back to Herod, they returned to their country by another route.*
>
> *When they had gone, an angel of the Lord appeared to Joseph in a dream. "Get up," he said, "take the child and his mother and escape to Egypt. Stay there until I tell you, for Herod is going to search for the child to kill him."*
>
> —Matthew 2:11-13

Okay, the Bible says the wise men came to the house, not a stable. Also, it says that as soon as they left, an angel appeared to Joseph and told them to leave as Herod was looking for the child.

We also know that Herod had every male child that was under two years of age killed, so we can assume that Jesus would have been two years old when the wise men showed up. But why did they show up?

WHY DID THE WISE MEN SHOW UP?

In a simple explanation, it was to bring them the wealth and provision needed for Joseph and Mary to carry out their assignment of raising Jesus, the Son of God. They were also about to leave on a very long journey, one in which they did not know when they would return, and they would also need provision for that period of time. God never gives us an assignment without the provision to carry it out. A quote from *Christmas, the Rest of the Story* by Rick Renner will give you an idea regarding what the wise men brought:

GOD NEVER GIVES US AN ASSIGNMENT WITHOUT THE PROVISION TO CARRY IT OUT.

> There is an assumption that there were three Magi who brought three gifts of gold, frankincense, and myrrh. But the facts prove this is at least partially incorrect, for the Magi would have brought a massive catalog of treasures to Jesus, not just three gifts of gold, frankincense, and myrrh.

No, this provision wasn't like packing a sandwich for a day hike. This was wealth and went beyond mere provision.

We also see this same principle when the slaves left Egypt. When the slaves left Egypt, they took with them all the gold and silver they could carry. They were launching a new nation, and it would take finances to accomplish all there was to do.

So, what did He give the church, you and me, to accomplish our mission? How would we be able to occupy the earth realm without finances? We wouldn't. God always pays the way!

When Peter, James, and John were called into the ministry in Luke 5, they started out with two boats so full of fish that the boats were almost sinking. I am sure they sold that fish and carried that money with them.

God always provides for His assignments.

When He called me to go to the nations in Albania, He said this to me:

> "I am calling you to the nations to teach My people My covenant of financial blessing. And wherever I send you, **I will pay for it**."

So, what did He give the church to carry out its mission?

To give you a simple answer, let me ask you a question. What did Adam lose when he sinned, which Satan now claims that he controls, according to Luke 4? Authority and splendor. We have talked about our authority over Satan in most of this book. I think that is very clear, but what about the splendor? To find out, let's go back to our key prophecy in Isaiah.

> *They will be called oaks of righteousness, **a planting of the Lord for the display of his splendor**.*
> —Isaiah 61:3b

Now, God was not talking about oak trees here, although they do have a splendor about them. He was talking about us. The "they" in that Scripture is us. He was saying that you and I are going to carry that splendor around for all to see. In a sentence, God has given us the splendor of the world to carry out our assignments. That should cover the bills, right?

He has given us the wealth of the nations to carry out our assignments.

Let me translate what that Scripture is saying to you and me: "Whatever it costs!" I can remember when the Powerball lottery jackpot reached one billion dollars, and some of the staff were saying how they were going to put a little toward that. You already know what they were saying, "Well, someone has to win it." I do not play the lottery, but a couple of guys were going out to buy a few tickets for those that wanted to participate; and I put in, I think, five dollars. That night, I had a dream where God told me this:

> "You do not need to play the lottery. All My promises are yours, and if you needed a billion dollars, I would get it to you."

Okay, I heard that loud and clear. I did not win the lottery, but I have a better, more secure source of revenue that is available to fund my assignments.

I also remember when we first launched daily TV. At the time, we were still doing a lot of work upgrading equipment and finishing out areas at the Now Center. Money was tight. We were just barely paying the airtime for our weekly TV broadcast when, in a prayer meeting at church, my daughter Amy began to prophesy the following words:

"The harvest is too big for you. I am stretching you. Only by My Spirit can you understand what is about to happen. Will you step out? Let Me lead you to hard things beyond your understanding, the impossible."

Wow. Like you, I do not like impossible things or hard things, but I have served the Lord long enough to say yes and figure it out later. Well, it was probably a week or two later when Daystar called us and offered us a daily time slot on their network. In the natural, it was impossible. Our airtime cost would instantly go five times higher. In other words, we were paying for one weekly time slot then, but we would be buying five days' worth of airtime instead of one. But after receiving that word and some encouragement from Drenda, we said yes. The money did pick up some when we went on daily, but we were falling behind. Before long, we were $500,000 behind on our airtime bills. That was not good, especially when your program is called *Fixing the Money Thing*. Our TV buyer called and asked me about the outstanding payments. He said his attorneys were getting a little nervous. Well at that moment, I began to think that maybe I should cut back on the TV airtime and cut costs.

But Drenda kept reminding me of what God said: "He would pay for it." I will have to admit, I struggled with the weight of that money I owed for about two weeks; and every time I would mention it to Drenda, she simply had one answer, "What did God say?" After attending a prayer meeting and having a few pastors pray with me, I finally felt peace. It was going to be okay.

I went home, and God gave me a dream. I saw a big pile of checks, and I even saw the names on the checks as well. When I woke up, I knew it was over. God was sending the money; I could relax. Sure enough, on the following weekend, over $500,000 came in during our normal offering. I hadn't even mentioned the situation or made a plea for the money to the church.

So, God's answer to me and to you is: "Whatever it takes." He will show you how to capture the money you need for any assignment you may be called to.

Let's go back to that prophecy in Isaiah 61 and take another look at it. If we look at the prophecy beginning in verse 1, we see that Jesus said He was anointed to preach good news to the poor. Boy, I usually get some pushback on that when I tell people that it really means what it says, with

> HE WILL SHOW YOU HOW TO CAPTURE THE MONEY YOU NEED FOR ANY ASSIGNMENT YOU MAY BE CALLED TO.

strange interpretations like, "Well, He meant poor in spirit." No, He meant, "God's Kingdom is great news to the poor." Why? Because they do not have to be poor any longer; there is a way of escape. Of course, the way of escape is this new covenant. But what I want to point out to you is a phrase that would have made the Jews in Jesus's day weep for joy if they would have believed Him. But instead, they wanted to kill Him over it. Here is what Jesus said:

> *Then he rolled up the scroll, gave it back to the attendant and sat down. The eyes of everyone in the synagogue were fastened on him. He began by saying to them, "Today this scripture is fulfilled in your hearing."*
>
> —Luke 4:20-21

Okay, what was it in Isaiah 61 that He said He was fulfilling?

Let's start with the first verse of Isaiah 61 and add to it Luke 4:19.

> *The Spirit of the Sovereign Lord is on me… to proclaim the year of the Lord's favor.*

That is where He stopped, even though the text in Isaiah that He was reading did not stop there. In fact, the next word after favor in Isaiah is the word "and." So why did Jesus stop in the middle of a sentence? Because He wanted to make a point. He was saying that He was the fulfillment of that sentence, which was referring to the Year of Jubilee, the most holy year of every Jew's existence! **<u>His statement was saying that He was the Messiah</u>**! To them, that was blaspheme, and they reacted with righteous anger.

> *All the people in the synagogue were furious when they heard this. They got up, drove him out of the town, and took him to the brow of the hill on which the town was built, in order to throw him off the cliff. But he walked right through the crowd and went on his way.*
>
> —Luke 4:28-30

I need to take a few minutes to help you understand what the Year of Jubilee was and why it is so important to your financial freedom.

When Adam gave away his position of authority over the earth back in Genesis, the whole earth came under a curse, which is simply the absence of the blessing of God. Man became a survivor, and the Bible says that from that point on, man would have to eat by his own painful toil and sweat. I call it the painful toil and sweat earth curse system.

When that happened, God gave Adam a picture of what He would one day restore, and that picture was called the Sabbath day. On that day, man was commanded to stop painfully toiling and sweating and to take time to worship God.

Every seven years there was also a Sabbath year, where, again, man was commanded to stop working for an entire year. On that seventh year, all debt had to be forgiven as well. This all sounded great, but how would they be able to take an entire year off?

Hold on. It gets much better than this. Every fifty years was called the Year of Jubilee. Let's remember that the forty-ninth year was a Sabbath year, meaning that the year before the Year of Jubilee, all their debt was forgiven. So, they came into the Year of Jubilee with no debt. In the Year of Jubilee, all slaves were set free, and all land was given back to the original owners. This was a total restoration of freedom, and did I mention they also could not sow their crops in that fiftieth year? So, freedom from the painful toil and sweat system of labor, no debt, freed if a slave, and all land ownership restored. It was a complete reset! So here is the million-dollar question: How could they survive if they did not plant in the forty-ninth year, fiftieth year, and then had to wait for the crops to harvest in the fifty-first year? That is three years with no harvest!

> *You may ask, "What will we eat in the seventh year if we do not plant or harvest our crops?" I will send you such a blessing in the sixth year that the land will yield enough for three years. While you plant during the eighth year, you will eat from the old crop and will continue to eat from it until the harvest of the ninth year comes in.*
>
> —Leviticus 25:20-22

THAT ABILITY TO REST AND NOT HAVING TO WORRY ABOUT FINDING PROVISION WAS CALLED THE SABBATH REST.

That must have been quite a harvest in that sixth year if it was going to feed them for three years. That ability to rest and not having to worry about finding provision was called the Sabbath rest. So, they got to enjoy that Sabbath rest every seven days, every seven years, and the big granddaddy Sabbath rest, the Year of Jubilee. But what was the Sabbath rest all about?

> *Therefore do not let anyone judge you by what you eat or drink, or with regard to a religious festival, a New Moon celebration or a Sabbath day.* ***These are a shadow of the things that were to come;*** <u>***the reality, however, is found in Christ***</u>*.*
>
> —Colossians 2:16-17

The Bible says that these Sabbath days and years were a shadow of what was to come. They were simply a shadow, not the reality. If I showed you a picture of some cookies or you were actually eating some cookies, you would have to agree that there is a big difference. Jesus is the reality of those shadows! Are you in Christ? Then He is talking to you. There is now freedom from the earth curse system of painful toil and sweat. There is a way to live free from debt. Owning land was a picture of their financial freedom as they were an agricultural society. There would be no more slavery but freedom. And here is the confirmation that this is valid for the New Testament church:

> *There remains, then, a Sabbath-rest for the people of God;*
> *for anyone who enters God's rest also rests from their works, just*
> *as God did from his.*
>
> —Hebrews 4:9-10

This is New Testament, friend. This is ours! So, why did God rest? Was He tired?

> *Thus the heavens and the earth were **completed** in all their vast array.*
>
> *By the seventh day God had **finished** the work he had been doing; so on the seventh day he rested from all his work. Then God blessed the seventh day and made it holy, because on it **he rested** from all the work of creating that he had done.*
>
> —Genesis 2:1-3

God was not tired; He was finished. Everything was complete on the seventh day of creation. Man was created at the end of the sixth day of creation and was designed to live in the seventh day, where everything was finished and everything was complete. But Adam lost that rest when he rebelled against God. Everything was then incomplete, and it produced the need for man to run after provision with constant anxiousness and fear. Man lost sight of his purpose and who he was. Survival ruled his thoughts. We were all born under that same earth curse system.

If I told you that you had to get out of debt, you would immediately begin to compute how to add more painful toil and sweat to your day to pay for that. That is the system we were all raised under. But Jesus has now come and has given us back that seventh day of rest with everything complete. I know. You are asking,

"How is that possible? That is not what I see out there." Let me go on.

Do you remember the manna that Israel ate in the wilderness? It would come down in the morning like the dew, and the people would gather it. But it would never last overnight; it would rot. They had to gather it every morning for that day's meals. But on the sixth day of the week, however, the manna did not rot, and they were instructed to keep it overnight for the Sabbath as there would be no manna on the Sabbath day to collect. Hold on. We are getting really close to the moment in the story where you let out a very loud Halleluiah. Let me show you what Moses said to the nation of Israel regarding the manna.

> He said to them, "This is what the Lord commanded: 'Tomorrow is to be a day of sabbath rest, a holy sabbath to the Lord. So bake what you want to bake and boil what you want to boil. Save whatever is left and keep it until morning.'"
>
> So they saved it until morning, as Moses commanded, and it did not stink or get maggots in it. "Eat it today," Moses said, "because today is a sabbath to the Lord. You will not find any of it on the ground today. Six days you are to gather it, but on the seventh day, the Sabbath, there will not be any."
>
> Nevertheless, some of the people went out on the seventh day to gather it, but they found none. Then the Lord said to Moses, "How long will you refuse to keep my commands and my instructions? Bear in mind that the Lord has given you the Sabbath; that is why on the sixth day he gives you bread for two days. Everyone is to stay where they are on the seventh day; no one is to go out." So the people rested on the seventh day.
>
> —Exodus 16:23-30

How was the Sabbath possible?

THE DOUBLE PORTION

The sabbath rest **was only possible by the double portion**, which means more than enough. As we have read, Jesus is our Jubilee and He is our Sabbath. And according to Hebrews 4:9, that rest, that double portion, is still ours today. In fact, the prophecy from Isaiah that we read earlier says the same thing in regard to the double portion.

> *You will feed on the wealth of nations, and in their riches you will boast. Instead of your shame **you will receive a double portion**, and instead of disgrace you will rejoice in your inheritance. And so you **will inherit a double portion in your land**, and everlasting joy will be yours.*
>
> —Isaiah 61:6b-7

There is another powerful truth in that prophecy in Isaiah 61 that we need to discuss. Do you remember when Jesus stood in His hometown and said, *"Today this scripture is fulfilled"*?

> *To proclaim the year of the Lord's favor **and** the day of vengeance of our God, to comfort all who mourn, and provide for those who grieve in Zion—to bestow on them a crown of beauty instead of ashes, the oil of joy instead of mourning, and a garment of praise instead of a spirit of despair. They will be called oaks of righteousness, **a planting of the Lord for the display of his splendor**. They will rebuild the ancient ruins and*

restore the places long devastated; they will renew the ruined cities that have been devastated for generations. Strangers will shepherd your flocks; foreigners will work your fields and vineyards.

And you will be called priests of the Lord, you will be named ministers of our God. You will feed on the wealth of nations, and in their riches you will boast. Instead of your shame you will receive a double portion, and instead of disgrace you will rejoice in your inheritance. And so you will inherit a double portion in your land, and everlasting joy will be yours.

—Isaiah 61:2-7

Do you remember that I said He stopped in the middle of the sentence?

To proclaim the year of the Lord's favor **and** *the day of vengeance of our God.*

Your prosperity is a weapon against the devil and his kingdom. God says you are to be an oak of righteousness for the display of His splendor. When you are out on a dark night, you do not have to look for the stars. They catch your attention; they shine so bright. In the same way, your prosperity will catch the attention of those in the world who are running after survival every day. This double portion will stand out to those that watch you!

Listen, friend, paying your bills is great. Don't misunderstand me. That's a great place to start, but if I took a poll, I would not be surprised if a lot of people reading this book today are still paying debt, still have mortgages, still have car payments. The sad thing is they have not been taught who they really are, who they really are legally in the Kingdom.

Peter, James, and John, in Luke 5, were fishermen their entire lives. They had fished that night and hadn't caught a thing. You remember the story. Jesus said to Peter, "Let me borrow your business. Let me borrow your boat," which he did. As you know, both boats in the business about sank with fish. The Bible says that they were astonished, and they **left everything else to follow Jesus**.

Now, I wonder why they would do that. If you had labored all night and caught nothing, then someone came along and showed you a system that would fill your boats and meet all your needs to overflowing capacity, I think you'd leave your boats behind as well, right? Friend, your prosperity is a lure to people. It speaks before you speak. It speaks before people know your name. God wants to use you. I'm not talking about materialism. Sure, there's a lot of ways to demonstrate God's goodness, but the bottom line is when you do not have money, when you are in debt, working at a job you hate, you don't have peace. And you won't have peace unless you're free.

See, if you're not free, your thoughts are consumed with tomorrow's bills; and God wants you free from that. You need to be about your assignment. God wants to show you how to prosper in a big way, yet you stay free in the process. You have more than enough, and you can share with people, be generous, because it speaks of God's goodness.

But is this really for today? Yes, it is, and let me tell you how God confirmed this truth to me.

CHAPTER NINE

DID THAT REALLY HAPPEN?

The double portion is yours. Jesus is your Sabbath rest, and He is your double portion! If you have read any of my previous books, you know that the Lord taught me a lot about the Kingdom through deer hunting. In fact, deer hunting was the vehicle that God used to catch my attention with the Kingdom. I had been deer hunting for a number of years with no success. Although I was putting time and money into my efforts, I ended up with no success and no venison. To be quite honest, I never even had a shot. This particular year, as I was thinking about the upcoming deer hunting season, God spoke to me and said, "Why don't you let Me help you with your deer hunting this year?" Of course, I had no idea what that meant, but He told me to take a check, write "for my 1987 buck" in the memo section, along with a certain amount of money, and then mail it to a ministry He directed me to send it to. He also said for Drenda and me to lay our hands on that check and claim Mark 11:24 as we prayed over it.

Mark 11:24 says,

Therefore I tell you, whatever you ask for in prayer, believe that you have received it, and it will be yours.

To make a long story short, I went out to a totally unfamiliar piece of property that year and had my buck in about 40 minutes. Drenda and I have followed these steps for the last 30 years, and I have always harvested my deer in 30 to 40 minutes every year since. Through the years, I have seen God do some pretty amazing things while out hunting, and I learned quite a few lessons about the laws of the Kingdom through hunting as well.

(All of those early stories are recorded in my *Faith Hunt* book.)

I usually prefer to bow hunt in the fall, with its warm colors, than to hunt in the cold gun season here in Ohio. The limit on the number of deer you can harvest is quite generous in Ohio, and in any given year, the limit is six deer a year. I have never had to harvest that many deer to feed my family. My freezer is usually pretty full with two or three deer a year. To appreciate what I am about to tell you, you need to know that while hunting all those years, I had never shot two deer from the same tree in the same morning or evening hunt. By the way, if you are not a hunter, yes, we bow hunt from a tree stand. Typically, when I killed a deer, I would leave the woods and come back out another day and take another one. But the Lord wanted to teach me something on this particular evening hunt.

It was one of those perfect fall hunting days; a bit of cloud cover and a light drizzle dampened the ground from time to time. It was a Sunday evening, and I was a bit tired from conducting multiple church services that morning. I was looking forward to being in the woods. Drenda was heading out to do some shopping for a few things, and she and I had agreed that this would be a good night to put some venison in the freezer. I was putting my camo on and gathering up my things as she went out to the car. I came outside just as she was starting the car to pull out. As she started the car, she rolled down the window and said to me, "The double portion." I did not know why she said that, although later, she said that she heard the Lord say that to her at that moment and felt led to tell me that.

We had sown for three deer that year, and this was the first day out hunting for that season. I gave her a quick kiss and told her I agreed, and I headed out toward our woods. I hunt on my own property, so I was very familiar with where I was headed.

As I climbed up into my tree stand, I gave my grunt call a couple of blows. Within 15 minutes, a large 8-point came running in. I took a 40-yard shot, and my buck was down. That was awesome! I climbed down and walked out to the buck, but then I remembered what Drenda had said—the double portion.

So, I left the buck where he had fallen, walked back to my tree, and climbed back up into the stand. I thought with all the commotion that I had made getting down, walking around, and then walking back to the stand and climbing up, let alone all the scent I had probably scattered around in that area, there would be a slim chance of another kill in the few remaining minutes of legal shooting light. But within 15 minutes of being in the tree, a button buck walked directly under my tree, and I dropped him with a perfect shot. Wow, two shots and two deer in a row from the same tree. I had never done that before. That caught my attention, and I knew it was the double portion Drenda had spoken of.

For the next three years, I had the same experience. Every time I went out bow hunting, I would get two deer out of the same tree minutes apart. I knew this was not normal. I began to dwell on the double portion, realizing that once again God was teaching me another lesson about His Kingdom.

I have always loved guns, and, of course, I love to hunt. I have my own collection of guns that I use for hunting, and I was pretty happy with the guns I owned. Drenda and I have 60 acres of land with about 25 acres of woods and another 15 acres of marsh. In any given fall, the marsh can be dry or full of water, depending on how wet the summer was. This particular year we had quite a wet summer, so the marsh was full of water as the fall duck season came in. There were always ducks coming into the marsh any year there was water, but I had not really paid much attention to them.

But this year, there were large flocks coming into the marsh with the water being so high. I could not resist. Although I had never set out to hunt them in the past, I thought I would go down to the marsh and try some duck hunting. Well, the hunting was great. There were ducks everywhere, and I had a few duck dinners that year.

While hunting ducks that year, I found that many times the ducks were passing just out of shotgun range. I was using my everyday all-around shotgun I usually used for rabbits and pheasants, but as the ducks flew just outside of shotgun range, I remembered that I had heard of a newer type of shotgun that was designed just for duck hunting. They were camouflaged and were able to shoot the new duck loads that carried a much larger load of shot, enabling much longer shots. I remember thinking I should check into them sometime.

Well, it just happened that I was in a local sporting goods store a month after the duck season ended when I spotted a rack of guns labeled waterfowl guns. I looked at them for bit, but with a $2,000 price tag and the fact that I would not need the gun for another 10 months when duck season reopened, I decided to wait on the purchase. Then without thinking, I said out loud, "Lord, I would like that one."

I did not think much about it as I left the store, but a few weeks later, I was speaking at a corporate sales meeting (not a church meeting, a corporate sales meeting). At the end of my presentation, the CEO thanked me for speaking and said, "We wanted to thank you for speaking tonight with a gift." I was in shock as he brought out the exact shotgun I had looked at in the sporting goods store only a few weeks earlier. My words, "Lord, I'll take that one" and the fact that I had given guns away in the past brought that harvest. That gun showing up was amazing for sure. It is not the real story I want to focus on, but it did prompt the story I want to tell you.

One day, after that gun showed up and I realized how I had put that harvest into motion, I thought for a moment about any other guns I would like to own. I had sown dozens of guns after all, so I thought I would experiment with the laws of the Kingdom. The only gun that I did not have in my collection was an over and under shotgun. They are beautiful shotguns, and usually, they are not cheap either. So, I said, "Lord, I would like to have one of those nice over and under shotguns!" About a month later, I received a call from a partner of the ministry. He said that he wanted to buy me a shotgun, an over and under, and he said he would be sending it by mail. I was thrilled.

Well, a few days later, I received two beautiful over and under shotguns in the mail, just gorgeous! Notice that I received two shotguns. *Wow*, I thought. I called the partner up and thanked him for the beautiful shotguns he had sent. In a few days, he sent two more. When I called to thank him again, he said, "I was so impressed that you actually called me personally to thank me, I wanted to send you two more." I was overwhelmed by the gifts, but I was beginning to see a pattern—two shotguns each time. Sounds like the double portion.

About two months later, I was teaching at a church in the morning, and then I was to teach in the same city at a different church that night. After the morning service, a man walked up to me and told me that he was impressed to send me a beautiful Browning semi-automatic shotgun he had. Again, I was thrilled. And he did send it the following week. Strangely, in the evening service at the other church, a man walked up and said, "I brought a brand-new rifle that is still in the box that I want to give you." It was a beautiful, scoped out Marlin 30/30, a gun that I have often admired but have never owned. Again, I was surprised, but I was catching on—the double portion.

A few weeks after that weekend, the same thing happened again: two shotguns were given to me on the same day. Then, when I was teaching this principle at a conference I was holding, two more guns showed up, always in pairs. Okay, I then knew that God was trying to tell me something.

During the same time these shotguns were showing up, another story was happening. This story has to do with our vehicles. Drenda and I are not really into cars. We usually just drive them until they stop working or just do not look good. But during a women's conference we held at Faith Life Church, we rented a Cadillac Escalade to drive the guests around. It was the first Escalade that I had ever driven, and we both said, "We like this." So, I said to Drenda, "I think we should get one of these. Do you like this shorter version, or do you think the longer version is better?" We both agreed the shorter one would be better. Then, we both agreed that we liked the pearl white color, which was the color of the rental we were driving. That's all. That is all we said. We did not tell anyone we said it, and we did not start looking for one either. But a couple of weeks after the conference, I picked up my cell phone, and a man on the other end said, "I want to buy you an Escalade. What color do you like?" We were not really expecting someone to just call us up and say they wanted to buy us one. But that is what happened. This man bought us a pearl white, short version Escalade, and it was and is just awesome. I love it.

One day, I noticed that the check engine light came on. *No big deal*, I thought, but I wanted to have it checked out, so I had a dealer take a look at it. They said it was not really an issue. The sensor was picking up a tiny bit of oil in the exhaust, but it would not cause a problem. The engine would last as long as I wanted to drive it. I asked them, "Why would it be picking up oil?" My escalade had a custom aftermarket exhaust system put on it, and they thought that could be the reason why it was picking it up. Again, they said the engine itself was fine, and I should expect the engine to last a long time.

In a casual conversation with the man that had given me the vehicle one day, I mentioned the sensor light issue I was having. He said, "Yes, I have seen that happen with some other GMC vehicles. In fact," he said, "it is quite common in the older ones." He went on to say that it would not affect the car in any way and that I should be able to drive the vehicle for the next 10 years or longer with no problem.

He knew that Drenda and I had a house in Florida that I had just purchased, and I sat there stunned as he then said, "I will tell you what. You drive this one down to Florida **WE KNEW IT WAS THE DOUBLE PORTION.** and use it down there, and I will buy you another one to drive up here in Ohio." Yes, I now have two pearl white, short version Escalades that are perfect in every way, besides the sensor light that comes on once in a while on the first one. They are both perfect in every way! Again, it was one of those, "Did you see that?" moments. Drenda and I have to pinch ourselves as we drive those beautiful vehicles. We did not pay for either one of those vehicles. But in this case, we knew it was the double portion.

I am not telling you these stories to brag in any way, but, friend, I am blessed! I have a gun safe full of guns, which I did not pay for; and now, I have two identical Escalades that I did not pay for.

And it is not that I am encouraging you to seek material things; I am not. I hold things loosely, and I do not worship stuff or pursue it. I pursue the King and His Kingdom, but in the Kingdom, I find more than enough—the double portion!

Wait, I am not done testifying of the Lord's goodness and the double portion just yet. I told the Lord that I was not really comfortable telling people what I had been given. But He told me, "I did this, you didn't, and I want you to tell people what I have shown you." So, let me continue.

I mentioned that house in Florida that I had purchased, and I need to tell you how that came about. Again, I am not bragging. I was and have been just as shocked as you are. My wife has wanted a beach home for the last 20 years. No, let me rephrase that: She has wanted one forever! She just loves the ocean! Anyway, she had been watching ocean property for years. In the past when there was a great deal on a home she liked, our money would be tied up in ministry projects, and we would wait. Well, that year, I was praying in the basement as I was riding my stationary bike. All of a sudden, the Lord impressed on me in a very strong way: "Tell Drenda to go to Florida, to that town she has desired to have a home in, and tell her to buy her ocean home this week." Wow! This week? There was a strong urgency in my spirit when I heard that.

So, I told Drenda what the Lord had said to me, and we contacted a friend of ours who lived in that city to see if she would want to drive Drenda around for a few days to look at houses. She said she would love to. Drenda went online and made a list of about 25 houses she wanted to take a look at. Once there, Drenda narrowed her list of 25 houses down to five that were a possibility and one that she said she loved. At that point, I flew down and joined her. She showed me the five houses and the one she loved. We narrowed the five to two, the one she loved and another house that was very nice but not as nice as the one she loved. I will have to admit when I saw the house that she loved, I knew it was Drenda's, and we ended up putting an offer on it. The owner accepted our offer, and we were then in contract to close on our new home.

A few weeks after we were in contract to buy the house, as we were home in Ohio just resting, Drenda gasped and said, "That's my house!" "I know," I said, "this is your house. God told me that I was to buy you your ocean home the week I sent you to the ocean." "No," she said, "you do not understand. That is my house." She went on to explain that she had been looking for homes in that area for a number of years, and one day, she saw a picture of the house we were buying in a real estate ad. When she saw it, she loved it. She loved everything about it, the Spanish Mediterranean architecture, the floor plan, the location, everything. She remembers putting her finger on that picture and saying, "Lord, I want that house!" She knew that house was too expensive, and we had already committed our cash to other projects, so she kept looking at houses that were in our price range at the time. But no other house clicked, and we never got to the point of actually putting a contract on one. We just did not have peace yet about a house.

You should also know that we had sown seed for an ocean beach house in this town over two years earlier. Our confession during this time was, "We have a beach house in this town. We already have it, and we received it the day that we sowed for it." I can remember the exact spot and moment that we held hands and came into agreement about Drenda's ocean beach house.

But then as we were in contract, Drenda suddenly remembered

the picture she had seen two years earlier and realized that this was the same house, her house! After investigating the history of the house, we found out that the owner had indeed tried to sell the house a few years earlier, but it did not sell, and he took it off the market. That was when Drenda had seen the picture of the house in the real estate listing. Then, the owner decided to list it again, and this explains why I had a sudden urgency to send Drenda to Florida with the instructions, "You are to buy a house this week." She will tell you that is not how I usually spend money. Timing is everything. This time, our money was not involved with other projects and was available for the house. I am sure that there were many people looking at that house, and that was the reason for the urgency. Amazingly, the price had not gone up from the price listed two years earlier when she first saw it. I believe God was holding it for her!

But here is the double portion part of the story. While our beach house was in contract, waiting to close, we received a call from Drenda's mother. Her parents owned a home in Canada for the last 36 years. Over the years, we had been there a number of times and loved the home and the location. The home is on an island right on the water. In fact, the ocean is about 30 feet from the back deck. Drenda's parents were getting older and decided that they did not want the upkeep and expense of a home that was so far away. They came to us and asked us if we had any interest in buying it, and I said no. It was a 31-hour drive from Ohio; and although I loved the place, I just did not see it being something that I could get to that often due to the travel time.

So, they listed the house with a real estate agent, but after having it on the market for two years, no buyer showed serious interest. So then, while we were waiting to close on our ocean beach house, they called and explained that they had tried to sell the home without success and would be willing to cut the price in half if we wanted to buy it and keep it in the family. As I thought about it, my children had grown up going there, and it is a beautiful place. Secondly, we then owned our own airplane, which would allow us to get there in four and a half hours. So, Drenda and I prayed about it and told her mother that we would take it. We had just enough cash on hand to make the purchase.

After we closed on both houses, I was sitting in my office one day when all of a sudden it hit me. Wait a minute; this is the double portion! My wife had been dreaming of an ocean home for years. But then in the space of two months, she got a home that is in the southern part of the United States, which is warm in the winter but too hot to really use much in the summer. The home in Canada is the perfect temperature in the summer but too cold in the winter. We realized that she now has an ocean house for both seasons. Incredible. We definitely said, "Did you see that?" when those two closings took place. I think you would agree this looks and smells like the double portion! Amazing!

I have used several examples of how God brought two of something to Drenda and me, which I believe God used to let us clearly see the double portion in operation. But I want to make sure that you do not think the double portion is limited to having two of something. In actuality, the double portion is simply having more than enough. God was using these very distinct examples of two of something to catch my attention about the double portion. So, no matter what it is, having it abundantly supplied is the double portion. I hope you are catching the reality of the double portion and the Sabbath rest. Life is so amazing in the Kingdom! As I write this chapter, I am sitting in our home in

Canada, looking out the window at the ocean. There are sea gulls and ducks playing along the shore only 25 yards from the house. There is peace, no striving. It is paid for and a blessing. I am on assignment, sharing the good news of my Father's Kingdom, a son in His house, a citizen of His great Kingdom, and I am enjoying the double portion!

Drenda and I could write so many stories of how the Kingdom of God and the laws that govern it have impacted our lives as well as the thousands of people that email us with their stories. As I said, you can read all these things in the Bible, but it is so exciting to see the Bible play out before your eyes.

Understand that I hate poverty with a passion. Those nine years of living in constant stress and fear were a living hell on earth, literally! I hope you will remember that the Sabbath rest is yours as well as mine! Just a side note to this chapter: As I just finished writing the above sentence, my secretary came into my office and said a box had arrived for me. I was surprised to open it and find two very nice shotguns. Wow, that was encouraging! It was just as if God was putting the amen on what I had just said.

There is so much I want to tell you in regard to finances, but I chose to tell you about the double portion, the Sabbath rest, in this book because you will need money to occupy your assignment. And instead of getting uptight or anxious about it, I wanted you to know that you can rest and know that God can handle it.

I asked God why He had all of these beautiful, expensive shotguns sent to me. After all, I did not need a whole gun safe full of them. And why the two Escalades? And I did not tell you about the two Louis Vuitton purses Drenda received on her birthday that year. And I did not tell you that we had gone to Quebec

City in Ontario, Canada, that Christmas. I was admiring all the gorgeous fur coats they had there. Being a trapper in my younger years, I always have admired furs. I remember telling Drenda that I would like to get her a fur coat one day. When we came home, there on our kitchen counter were two boxes. I was shocked to find a beautiful $5,000 black mink coat in each box. So, God spoke to me and said, "I know you do not need all those guns, but I am not limited to need. You own the whole estate. I sent you the top-of-the-line products because I want to stretch your capacity to receive from Me. I wanted you to understand that you have the double portion. There is no such thing as need in My Kingdom." Then, He said this, "I always send the double portion, but My people will not receive it! Their poverty mindset rejects it. But I have shown you My goodness. Now, go and tell others what I have shown you."

So, as I said earlier, God has given us the entire estate. There are no limits to His riches and glory. So, lift up your eyes and think bigger. Yes, your destiny will require people and money. But God will show you who, and He will provide the money.

YOU ARE CALLED TO OCCUPY and STAND IN GOD'S ASSIGNMENT FOR YOR LIFE! IT IS YOUR DESTINY!

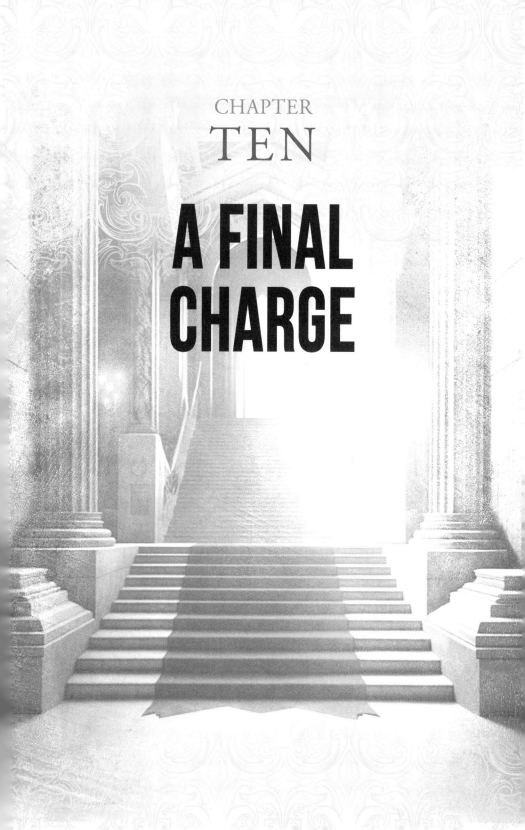

CHAPTER
TEN

A FINAL CHARGE

I have included the following two sections as appendixes. I included them because I think you need to know this information so you can succeed in your ability to occupy your destiny.

The first appendix deals with faith, what it is, why it is needed, and how to get faith.

The second appendix deals with the Baptism of the Holy Spirit and how to hear God. You will have many decisions on your journey, and the Holy Spirit will help you make the right ones.

I cannot emphasize enough just how much your success will be determined by the information I have included here.

I close with this last thought. It will take courage to stand face-to-face with Goliath. As Joshua was facing the task of leading the nation of Israel into a land with giants and walled cities, God gave him these commands:

- **Be strong and courageous.**
- **Do not be afraid.**
- **Do not be discouraged for the Lord your God will be with you wherever you go.**

FAITH
APPENDIX

What is faith?

Faith is a term that Christians throw around loosely. And I am convinced that many, if not the majority, do not know what faith is, why it is needed, how to know if they are in faith, and how to find faith. If faith is the switch that healed the woman in Matthew 9:20-22, as Jesus stated, then we need to take a very close look at faith! We find our definition of faith in Romans 4:18-21. Oh, I know what you are thinking, *No, Gary. Hebrews 11:1 is our definition of faith.*

> *Faith is being sure about what we hope for, convinced about things we do not see.*
>
> —Hebrews 11:1 (EHV)

Yes, that is the traditional answer, but if you look at the Scripture, Hebrews 11:1 is telling us the benefits of faith, not what faith actually is. I believe our Scripture in Romans will give us a very clear picture of what faith actually is.

> *Against all hope, Abraham in hope believed and so became the father of many nations, just as it had been said to him, "So shall your offspring be." Without weakening in his faith, he faced the fact that his body was as good as dead—since he*

was about a hundred years old—and that Sarah's womb was also dead. Yet he did not waver through unbelief regarding the promise of God, but was strengthened in his faith and gave glory to God, being fully persuaded that God had power to do what he had promised.

—Romans 4:18-21

Let's understand the setting of this story. Abraham and Sarah could not have children. I do not mean they were having trouble conceiving a child and should keep trying. I mean they were almost 100 years of age, and it was over. Their bodies could not have children; it was impossible! Yet God promised Abraham a child even though in the natural it was utterly impossible. The Bible says that Abraham was fully persuaded that God had the power to do what He said, in spite of the natural facts that stated a different story.

"FAITH IS BEING SURE ABOUT WHAT WE HOPE FOR, CONVINCED ABOUT THINGS WE DO NOT SEE."
—HEBREWS 11:1 (EHV)

Here then is our definition of faith: "being fully persuaded that God has the power to do what He has promised." I state it this way: **Being in agreement with heaven,** not just mentally but fully persuaded, our hearts settled and convinced totally of what God has said, in spite of the natural realm indicating something else.

Our definition of what faith is:

Faith is being fully persuaded of what God says! It is our hearts and minds being in agreement with heaven, our hearts being fully persuaded, confident, and at rest.

Why is faith needed?

Why can't God just heal everyone in the hospital when He wants to? Why can't He stop wars? Why can't He send angels to preach the Gospel to us? I am sure you have heard all of these questions before. The answer is that He can't. It is not that God does not have the ability to do so. He does not have the jurisdiction or the authority to do so. "Gary, are you saying that God cannot do whatever He wants to?" I know this sounds really strange to you right now, but let's look at the Bible to find our answer to that one.

> But there is a place where someone has testified:
> "What is man that you are mindful of them, a son of man that you care for them? You made them a little lower than the angels; you crowned them with glory and honor and put everything under their feet."
> In putting everything under them, God left nothing that is not subject to them. Yet at present we do not see everything subject to them.
>
> —Hebrews 2:6-8

We can see from this Scripture that God gave man complete legal jurisdiction over the entire earth realm when he was placed here. There was nothing that was not under his jurisdiction. He ruled over this realm with absolute jurisdiction and authority. His ability to rule with authority was backed up by the government which had set him here. In essence, he ruled with the delegated authority of the Kingdom of God. He wore the crown of that government, which represented the glory of God, the anointing, and the position of honor that he bore.

To get a good picture of what this looks like, think of a natural king. Although he is a natural man and bears no real power in his natural being, he wears a crown that signifies he stands in representation of not only himself but also an entire kingdom and government. His words carry authority only because they are backed up by all the power and natural resources of the government and kingdom he represents.

If you think of a sheriff directing traffic, he will stop a massive tractor-trailer truck with a command, "Stop in the name of the law." Yes, the truck is much bigger than the man, and the man, in himself, is no match for the truck, but the truck stops. It stops not because of the man but because of the badge the man wears, which represents a government. In this case, the government is much bigger than the man who wears the badge. For the truck driver, there is no fear of the man, but there is a fear of the government that the man represents, causing the truck to stop.

The same is true here. Adam ruled over everything that was created in the earth realm. God's power and dominion, represented by the crown of glory and honor, gave man the assurance that his words ruled on behalf of the Kingdom of God.

It is very important to note that when Adam lost his ability to rule over the earth by committing treason against God's government, he lost his crown. The earth realm became tainted and changed. Death entered the earth realm, and Satan then had a legal claim of authority and influence in the affairs of men. It is imperative that you also understand that man is still the legal ruler over the earth realm, as God has placed him in that position, but he now has no authority to rule spiritually as he once had. Even in his fallen state, however, he is still in charge of the earth. Yes, he no longer has his crown of God's government to back him up. He has no authority to rule with God's power and glory; he has lost his position of honor. But he is still the only legal door to the earth realm. This is why God has to use Spirit-filled people to bring about His will in the lives of men.

> **THIS IS WHY GOD HAS TO USE SPIRIT-FILLED PEOPLE TO BRING ABOUT HIS WILL IN THE LIVES OF MEN.**

In the same way, Satan uses demon-inspired people to affect the earth realm toward his plan for man. This principle of man's jurisdiction over the earth is vital to your understanding of Kingdom law, and once you understand it, it will answer many questions you may have in the future as to why certain things happen, or why certain things did not or do not happen spiritually.

You may say, "But I thought God owned the earth and the fullness thereof?" True, He does. I hope this example will help you understand what I am saying. If I leased a home that I owned to you, although I legally owned the home, I legally gave up the right to drop by anytime I wanted to. There is a clause in most leases that specifies when landlords may legally enter rented premises—for example, to deal with an emergency or to make repairs—and the amount of notice required. If I tried to enter the home outside of this agreement, it would be considered breaking and entering, even if I owned the property. If I violated the law specified in the lease, I could then be legally forced to vacate the premises even though I owned it. This illustrates why Satan had to go through Adam to gain access to the earth realm. Only Adam had the key! Satan had to go through the door, and Adam was it. If Satan tried to go around Adam, he would have legally been forced out.

> *The devil led him up to a high place and showed him in an instant all the kingdoms of the world. And he said to him, "I will give you all their authority and splendor, for it has been given to me, and I can give it to anyone I want to. So if you worship me, it will all be yours."*
>
> —Luke 4:5-7

You can see in this verse that Satan claims that the authority and splendor (wealth) of the kingdoms of men have been given to him. Who gave him this authority? The one who had it, Adam! Thus God cannot just burst into the affairs of men without going through a legal entrance. If He did, Satan would claim foul play. No, God would have to go through the same door that Satan used to bring His government and authority to bear in the earth, and that was a man. But was there such a man?

> *The Lord had said to Abram, "Go from your country, your people and your father's household and go to the land I will show you. I will make you into a great nation, and I will bless you; I will make your name great, and you will be a blessing. I will bless those who bless you, and whoever curses you I will curse; and all peoples on earth will be blessed through you."*
>
> —Genesis 12:1-3

Abraham is called the father of our faith because he is the man that opened the door of the earth realm to God whereby all nations on the earth would be blessed. Of course, when this verse speaks of the nations being blessed, it is speaking of Jesus Christ, who would later make a way for the government of God to once again have legal access to the earth realm through the faith of Abraham.

Abraham's faith opened a legal doorway for heaven, which God locked permanently open by making a legal agreement (covenant) with Abraham and his seed or heirs.

"CONSEQUENTLY, FAITH COMES FROM HEARING THE MESSAGE, AND THE MESSAGE IS HEARD THROUGH THE WORD ABOUT CHRIST."
—ROMANS 10:17

Let me paraphrase what I am saying. The government of heaven can only gain its access into the earth realm through a man or a woman on the earth because they have legal jurisdiction there. That legality can only be accomplished if a man or woman is totally persuaded in their heart of what God says (faith).

Another way to say it is that heaven can only legally affect a man or woman in the earth realm who desires and chooses to come under God's dominion and authority. This would be the same principle that Satan used to gain access into the earth, using Adam to do so. He convinced Adam that God could not be trusted and brought Adam's heart out of agreement with God. Consequently, Adam chose to believe Satan and rejected God's authority.

This is the same principle that God would then use to bring His government and authority back into the earth realm through Abraham. Abraham believed God, and his agreement was counted by God as righteousness, meaning that the required legal agreement was there. This agreement by both parties, God and Abraham, allowed God to put a legal contract (a covenant) in place that secured heaven's access into the earth realm, BUT it is vital to note that this agreement only affected Abraham and his heirs. A sign of this covenant was given to all of Abraham's heirs, which was circumcision. Circumcision was the cutting off of the foreskin from the male penis. As a man planted his seed in a woman, his seed had to pass through that circumcised penis, which declared to Satan and the father and mother themselves that this child stood before heaven as an heir of that legal agreement that God and Abraham had put in place.

As we read previously, however, each man or woman, although having that legal agreement <u>available</u> to them, still had to fulfill the legal requirement of their own heart being fully persuaded of what God said to actually enjoy the personal benefits of that agreement that God and Abraham made. In essence, the covenant ran the power lines to their house, but they still had to turn on the switch by believing and acting on the Word personally.

Okay, we now know what faith is and why faith is legally required. It is now imperative that we know how to get faith and how to know if we are in faith.

How do we get faith?

Here is a clue: You can't pray for faith. Surprised? I thought so.

> *Consequently, faith comes from hearing the message, and the message is heard through the word about Christ.*
> —Romans 10:17

How does faith come by hearing the Word of God? Is that all there is to it? What is the process? Is just hearing the Word all it takes for faith to be developed in the human spirit? To understand how faith comes and what Romans 10:17 is talking about, we can look to Mark chapter 4. If you throw your Bible up in the air, it should land open to Mark chapter 4; it is that important! Jesus said in Mark 4:13 that if you did not understand what He was teaching in this chapter, you would not be able to understand any other parable in the Bible. I would say that is pretty important!

Why is this chapter so important? It is because it tells us how heaven interfaces into the earth realm, how it gains legality, and where that takes place. Nothing is more important to your life than knowing what this whole chapter is talking about. "How does the Kingdom of God operate?" you may ask. Read Mark chapter 4! In this chapter, Jesus tells us three parables regarding how faith is produced in the human spirit, which as you know now, is a requirement for heaven to legally invade Earth.

The three stories in this chapter are the parable of the sower, the parable of the man scattering seed, and the story of the mustard seed.

Let's begin by first looking at the second story Jesus tells in Mark chapter 4, the story of the man scattering seed.

> He also said, "This is what the Kingdom of God is like. A man scatters seed on the ground. Night and day, whether he sleeps or gets up, the seed sprouts and grows, though he does not know how. All by itself the soil produces grain—first the stalk, then the head, then the full kernel in the head. As soon as the grain is ripe, he puts the sickle to it, because the harvest has come."
> —Mark 4:26-29

Before we jump into this passage, let's first define our terms. What is the seed Jesus is talking about, and what is the ground? Jesus actually defines those terms in the preceding parable of the sower in the same chapter. The seed is the Word of God, and the ground is the heart of man or the spirit of man. So in this parable, using Jesus's own definition of those two words, we would say that Jesus is saying a man scatters the Word of God into his own heart. Then all by itself the soil or the heart of man starts to produce faith (agreement with heaven) in the earth realm.

Before I go forward, it is critical that you remember what our definition of faith is: the heart of a man or woman firmly persuaded of what heaven says. This passage says that although the man does not know how the process works, the Word that was sown into his heart begins to grow and produce agreement all by itself. This happens if he sleeps or is awake; it does not matter, the process continues. As the man keeps the Word in his heart, slowly his heart is coming into agreement with what heaven says, and faith is being produced.

Our Scripture reference in Mark chapter 4 tells us that the heart produces agreement through a process. The story tells us that at first when our heart receives the Word, faith begins to form. Jesus compares that phase to a sprout. The sprout then goes on and continues to grow and becomes a stalk. Eventually, the head forms on the stalk, but even at this late phase, there is no fruit, no agreement, and no change in the natural realm. Then Jesus says the process continues as the head then matures and produces mature grain. When the process reaches that point, when the mature seed is in the head, agreement is there and faith is there, allowing the man or woman to harvest into the earth realm what heaven had planted in the heart of the man.

Now, pay close attention. Let's review what actually happened. Heaven sows the Word of God into the earth realm, into the heart of a man or woman where agreement is needed. At that time, the man's heart is not in agreement with heaven yet, but a process begins to take place in the heart that brings the heart, all by itself, into agreement with what was sown. Jesus uses a great illustration to show us this process. Comparing this process to a farmer sowing seed and how the plant matures, Jesus gives us a picture of what faith looks like. In the natural realm, when the seed in the head is mature, it will look **EXACTLY** like the seed that was sown into the ground. Let me say that again.

When the seed that is in the head of the plant matures, it will look exactly—EXACTLY—like the seed that was sown into the ground.

Plant a corn plant and the mature seed in the ear will match the seed that you planted. They are the same, look the same, and taste the same. You cannot tell the difference between the two; they are identical. So, let me paraphrase what Jesus is saying. When we hear the Word (Romans 10:17), we are actually scattering God's Word into our spirit men, our hearts. If we keep that Word in our hearts, it will mature; and when it is mature, the pictures in our hearts (the earth realm) will match what heaven says.

If we put it in different terms, we could say that as you sow a promise from heaven into your heart, it will slowly produce confidence of what God said all by itself. Eventually, your heart will be fully persuaded of what heaven says, and agreement will be there. For instance, if you are facing sickness, your circumstances in your body are speaking to you that you are sick. As you sow the Word of God that says that God has paid the price for your healing through what Jesus did, your heart slowly begins to become convinced of what God says all by itself.

When that Word matures in your heart, the confidence that you are healed becomes what **you** believe and say. No longer are you simply quoting what heaven says. Your heart is now firmly convinced. When you say, "I am healed," it is not a formula that you are quoting; rather, this is what you believe and know to be a fact. What heaven says has now become your own perception of reality.

This is why Hebrews 11:1 (EHV) says:

> *Faith is being sure about what we hope for, being convinced about things we do not see.*

There is a supernatural assurance of what heaven says when faith is there, yet there is still another step in the process.

The man now must put in his sickle to harvest, to bring into his actual realm of existence, what he is sure of in his heart.

> *As soon as the grain is ripe, **he puts the sickle to it**, because the harvest has come.*
>
> —Mark 4:29

Notice that even though the heart is in agreement with heaven, and heaven's reality has become the man or woman's reality, no real change has yet occurred in the physical realm. Because man is the one who naturally has jurisdiction here in the earth, he is the one who must also release that authority of heaven into this realm. God cannot do it without the man or woman. I can show you this in a very familiar Scripture.

> *For with the heart one believes and is **justified**, and with the mouth one **confesses** and is saved.*
>
> —Romans 10:10 (ESV)

With the heart man believes the Word, producing faith, and is justified. Justify is a legal term meaning the administration of law. So when a man's heart is in agreement with heaven, and his heart is fully persuaded of what heaven says, he is justified. It is then legal for heaven to flow into his life, into the earth realm. But being justified alone does not release the power of God. Like a house that has the power run to it from the power station, there is one more step—turning the switch on to release the power, and then the lights come on. Why? Because as Romans 10:10 points out, there is one more step after being justified.

A man or woman who stands before heaven and earth justified must then confess or act upon that agreement to actually release the power and anointing of God into the earth realm. Please read that Scripture again and then again until you completely understand what I am saying. This is how it works! This is how heaven gains legality in the earth realm—the heart is the interface of heaven in the earth realm, and then our words and actions are the switches that actually release heaven's power. Please pay close attention to the second part of that verse again: We are the ones who must release heaven's authority here.

The concept of heaven waiting on a man or woman to, first of all, provide legality and, secondly, jurisdiction in the earth realm can be seen through what Jesus taught in Matthew 16:19 and Matthew 18:18.

> *I will give you the keys of the kingdom of heaven; whatever you bind on earth will be bound in heaven, and whatever you loose on earth will be loosed in heaven.*
>
> —Matthew 16:19

Truly, I say to you, whatever you bind on earth shall be bound in heaven, and whatever you loose on earth shall be loosed in heaven.

—Matthew 18:18 (ESV)

Jesus states in Matthew 16:19 that He is going to give the church the keys (authority) of the Kingdom of heaven in the earth realm. He said that whatsoever you bind on earth, heaven will back up, and whatsoever you loose on earth, heaven will back up. Again, think of a police officer; he has the authority, but the government has the power. The police officer holds the key or the authority of the government, as he was sworn in to be an agent of that government. What he says, the government backs up. Remember, only a man or woman has legal jurisdiction here, and thus only a man or woman can give heaven legal jurisdiction here.

THIS IS HOW HEAVEN GAINS LEGALITY IN THE EARTH REALM—THE HEART IS THE INTERFACE OF HEAVEN IN THE EARTH REALM, AND THEN OUR WORDS AND ACTIONS ARE THE SWITCHES THAT ACTUALLY RELEASE HEAVEN'S POWER.

There is one more very important point that you need to know about faith. Let me reference our Scripture in Mark chapter 4 again for a moment.

*All by itself the **soil produces grain**—first the stalk, then the head, then the full kernel in the head.*

—Mark 4:28

Remember, Jesus defined the soil mentioned in this parable as representing the heart of man, or the spirit of man, as I mentioned before. Notice where faith is produced; does that surprise you? It is not a product of heaven, as most people believe, but it is produced here in the earth realm and is a product of your heart. You cannot pray for it or ask God for it. Faith is not needed in heaven. We will not need agreement in heaven. No, it is only required here in the earth realm, and it can only occur in the hearts of men and women on the earth. As the parable in Mark 4 teaches, there is only one way to get it—by putting the Word of God in your heart and letting the process of agreement take place. So if I need faith, what would I do? I would scatter the Word of God into my heart and let it grow until faith was there. That is the only way it comes.

Before I leave Mark 4, I want to talk about the sickle mentioned there again.

> *As soon as the grain is ripe, **he puts the sickle to it**, because the harvest has come.*
>
> —Mark 4:29

I believe that most of the church world has not been taught how to use the sickle, meaning they have not been taught how to harvest what they need. The church in general has been taught how to give but not how to cultivate and harvest from the seed they have sown. Jesus is very specific in this verse, saying that when the harvest of our faith is available, WE must put in the sickle. Even though we may have done a great job of releasing our seed in faith, unless we know how to put in the sickle, there will be no harvest. Quite frankly, I knew nothing about this either until the Lord began teaching me how the Kingdom operates. Let me give you a few examples of what this looks like.

I was invited to speak at a church in Atlanta. It was a Wednesday night service, and the church was not that big, but that was fine with me. I just loved teaching people about the Kingdom. As I arrived at the church, I found it strange that the doors were locked and no one was there. It was ten minutes before service was to begin. I heard a really loud truck behind me; it sounded like it had no muffler at all. As I looked over, I saw an old beat-up, broken-down pickup truck pulling into the alley behind the church. I thought nothing of it; after all, I was in downtown Atlanta. As I waited, a man came walking from behind the building and introduced himself as the pastor. He said he was sorry for being late, but his old truck would not start. He told me he had to start the truck by coasting it downhill then, once getting up some speed, popping the clutch since the starter was inoperative. He said many times it would not start at all, and he would have to walk the five miles to the church.

As he went on telling me about his church, he told me that although he was the pastor of the church, the church's main function was to feed inner city people. They fed over 10,000 meals a month at that location.

As the pastor was speaking, I was getting upset. Here was a man of God who was feeding 10,000 people a month, and he did not even have a reliable car? He was the only picture of God that many of those people he fed would ever see. If they saw him barely making it, having to walk to church five miles on a 100-degree summer day, what confidence would they have that God could help them? I could take care of that. I had a fairly young car with 20,000 miles on it at home that I could give him. I told him of my plan and that I would send one of my staff down to Atlanta with the car. He, of course, was thrilled. I spent that night teaching him and his small church about the Kingdom of God and how it functioned in relation to money.

When I went home, I arranged for the car to be driven to Atlanta. When my staff member came to my house to pick up the car, I knew that I was making a spiritual transaction in heaven. I knew that as I released that car into the Kingdom of God, I could believe God for a vehicle that I would have need of as well. As I mentioned, I am not a car person, meaning I am not really into cars. Some people are, but I am not. A car is just a tool to me. I like to have a nice car, of course, but I usually drive them until they need replaced.

When my staff member stopped by, I went out into my garage, and I laid my hands on that car and said, "Father, I release this car into the work of your ministry, and as I release this car, I receive back a car...." I hesitated. I know how specific the Kingdom of God is, and I knew that just the word "car" would not do. I also knew that I had to be specific and that Drenda and I needed to be in agreement concerning the specifics of what we received. As I stood there mid-sentence, I also realized that I had no idea what kind of car I wanted. So I started over, "Lord, today I release this car into your ministry, and I believe that I receive a really nice car as I sow, but I will have to get back to you on the model and type when I figure that out." That was it; the car was gone. I really did not have any car in mind that I could say, "Yes, I want THAT car."

A few months went by. Of course, Drenda was in agreement with me in giving the car away, and, like me, she did not have a clue what kind of car she wanted. Over the next two months, we talked about cars, and finally one day she said, "You know, I think I would enjoy having a convertible." I told her that I agreed and said

I thought that sounded fun, but what kind? Again, we did not even know what kind of convertibles were out there.

But one day as we were driving out to lunch, my wife suddenly said, "That's it!" "What's it?" I said. "That's it," she said as she was pointing across the parking lot of the restaurant we had pulled into. "What's it?" I said. "That car, that's the car I want!" I then saw a sharp convertible across the parking lot. "Let's go see what kind it is," I said. So we drove over to the car and pulled up behind it. Well, no wonder we liked it. It was a BMW 645Ci, a nice convertible for sure, and a very expensive one at that. To be honest with you, when I saw that make of car, I thought, *Okay, Lord, show us what to do.* I knew I was not going to pay $115,000 for a new BMW, but I also knew that God can do amazing things. Drenda and I did not tell anyone about the car or mention to anyone that we were looking for a car.

About two weeks later, Drenda's brother called us and said, "I found Drenda's car!" "What do you mean you found Drenda's car?" I said. He said, "I saw this car for sale, and all of a sudden, I just felt that this was supposed to be Drenda's car; and I was supposed to tell you about it." "What kind of car is it?" I asked. "It is a BMW 645Ci, and it is perfect; I mean perfect. It is a couple of years old, low mileage, and there is not a scratch on it. Besides that, you know the man who is selling it." "I do?" I said. "Yes. He said you should call him about it." Well, when he told me the car's make and model, knowing that it was the exact car that Drenda and I had said we both liked just a couple of weeks previously, I knew that God was up to something.

I called the man who owned the car. Yes, I did know him, and we talked a bit about the car, and he was telling me how great of a shape the car was in. And then he said these words to me. "You know, ever since we have been on the phone speaking about this car, I just really feel like this is supposed to be Drenda's car." I had not even mentioned to him that I was looking at the car for Drenda. The man went on and said, "I tell you what I am going to do. I am going to sell it to you for $28,000." I could hardly believe what my ears were hearing. The car was worth so much more than that. When I told Drenda about it, she was thrilled, to say the least. We paid cash for that car and still have it today. It still runs and looks great. There is still not a scratch on it, and we have taken many drives in that car with the top down, the stereo blaring, and the sun breathing life into a tired day.

Our favorite trip was driving that awesome convertible through the Colorado mountains, with our camping supplies in the trunk. Our daughter Kirsten was with us on that trip, and I remember driving through Kansas on I-70 during the night with the top down. Kirsten was lying in the back asleep as I drove. The stars shone so brightly over our heads, and the road was vacant except for an occasional truck or two. It was one of those perfect nights where the air was just right and all was wonderful in the world. We spent the next two weeks driving through the Rockies, and I found out just how great that car handled. One word can describe it—awesome!

But here is the one million-dollar question. How did that car get here? Why was it the exact car that Drenda said, "That's it!" about? I knew that the Kingdom of God brought that car into our lives. I knew that when I sowed that car to that pastor, I was putting spiritual law into place. I remember saying that I was receiving back a car, not an SUV, not a jeep, a car; I remember saying a nice one. But Drenda and I had to put the sickle in. That car would not have shown up until we said, "That's it!" Although I was in faith when I released that car, we had not put in the sickle until Drenda said, "That's it."

The incident I told you about in chapter nine brought out that principle in an even greater way. I was relating the story of the shotgun that was made just for duck hunting to a fellow minister friend of mine." He said, "Yes, I suppose God does that sometimes. He will just bless you with a special little gift to tell you He loves you." As I thought about what he said, I realized, "No, that is not right. Yes, God loves me, but He did not just want to surprise me with a little gift." The car and the gun had come not because God just wanted to show me He loved me. He showed me He loved me when He sent Jesus for me and gave me the Kingdom!

> **...GOD JUST WANTED TO SHOW ME HE LOVED ME. HE SHOWED ME HE LOVED ME WHEN HE SENT JESUS FOR ME AND GAVE ME THE KINGDOM!**

I have said for years that the church has done a fairly great job of teaching about giving but a horrible job of teaching people how to harvest. So, can you tell what the sickle is from the preceding stories? I hope it is obvious! The sickle is our words!

> *The tongue has the power of life and death, and those who love it will eat its fruit.*
>
> —Proverb 18:21

There was a season where the church seemed to teach a lot about our confession. I have been with people, and you may have also, that would say something and then cover their mouths and say, "I need to watch my confession." That sounds like a noble task, and I agree that will help keep the Word in your heart. However, watching your confession really has nothing to do with the sickle. What? But I thought you just said the sickle was our words. Yes, I did, but just mastering the formula of saying the right thing is not the key by itself.

> *Truly, I say to you, whoever* __*says*__ *to this mountain, "Be taken up and thrown into the sea," and does not doubt in his heart, but* __*believes*__ *that what* __*he says*__ *will come to pass, it will be done for him.*
>
> —Mark 11:23 (ESV)

Again, the sickle in Mark chapter 4 is your words! By the time Mark chapter 4 discusses the sickle, it has already discussed the process of faith and how to get it. It says when the seed is mature, you put in the sickle because the harvest has come. The harvest has come because you are in faith, agreeing with heaven in your heart. The above verse in Mark 11 bears out the same principle. Your heart believes the Word, then you speak and release heaven's authority. But notice the phrase, "*believes that what he says will come to pass.*" The test of faith is if you believe what you are saying. Just saying or confessing the Word of God is not faith by itself. Unless your heart is in agreement with heaven, you can confess until you are blue in the face and nothing will happen. So should you monitor your confession or your heart?

> *The good person brings what is good out of the good stored up in his heart, and the evil person brings what is evil out of the evil within. To be sure, what his mouth speaks flows from the heart.*
>
> —Luke 6:45 (EHV)

Above all else, guard your heart, for it is the wellspring of life. Put away perversity from your mouth; keep corrupt talk far from your lips.

—Proverbs 4:23-24 (BSB)

We can clearly see that what we say comes out of our hearts and what we believe. By following the process in Mark chapter 4, we know how to actually change what our hearts believe and bring them into alignment with heaven and in faith. Then when we are fully persuaded, we put the sickle in with our words and action. Got it? Great, let's move on.

As we continue our discussion on faith, I want to bring up a question that you must be able to answer.

How do I know if I am actually in faith?

That is a great question and one you **must** know since it is impossible to pray the prayer of faith without first being in faith. There are many ways to know if you are in faith or not, many symptoms that you need to know and to look for. You can make a lot of bad fear-based decisions when you are not in faith. Fear-based decisions will always hold you hostage to the earth curse and will cause you to miss out on what God wants for you.

So, what is the evidence of being in faith? The first sign is easy; you can look back at our definition of faith and understand that being fully persuaded in your heart is a real key. But many times we think we are persuaded but are only agreeing in our minds with the Word and not in our hearts. You need to be able to tell the difference. When you are fully persuaded, there is, of course, a mental agreement with what the Word says but also a knowing of being sure, a confidence that brings peace and expectation.

Faith is being sure about what we hope for, convinced about things we do not see.

—Hebrews 11:1 (EHV)

If you had evidence that you had something, would you still need to be reassured that you had it? Of course not. Again, when you are in faith, there is a knowing, a peace, and a confidence that you have what the Word of God says, even though you may not see it yet. Many people say it this way: "I know that I know that I know that I know I have it." This knowing is from the inside and not from what circumstances are telling you. It is in your spirit man or your heart. Fear is gone, no more nagging thoughts of worry bombard your mind; you know it is done.

Another aspect of being in faith is joy and expectation. Your answer is here. You have it! Faith is more than a feeling of peace or confidence, although you will have that. You should also be able to defend your position spiritually. When I say that, think of a courtroom and you as the attorney cross-examining the witness. Why do you believe what you believe about your situation? How would you defend your position? There is only one answer, the Word of God.

For instance, if someone came to your house and said, "Hey, get out of my house," would you say, "Oh, I am sorry; give us a day, and we will be out"? No, you wouldn't; you would probably laugh. If the fellow said, "No, this is my house; get out or I will see you in court," your reply would be, "I will gladly see you in court!" At the hearing, you would calmly show the judge your deed. He would take one look at it and arrest the other guy for harassment and make him pay all court costs. Your confidence was established not on how you felt and your emotions but, rather, on the law and the fact that you legally owned the house.

When it comes to being in faith, I find that many times people who do not understand what faith is are easily confused by putting

**"FAITH IS BEING SURE ABOUT WHAT WE HOPE FOR, CONVINCED ABOUT THINGS WE DO NOT SEE."
—HEBREWS 11:1 (EHV)**

their confidence in their actions instead of their only source of faith, which is the Word of God. It is easy to confuse the action or formula of acting on the Word of God with the real power of the Kingdom, which comes from a heart that is confidently persuaded. For instance, if you sowed money into the Kingdom of God, and I asked you why you believe you will receive a return on that giving, your answer should not be, "Because on such and such a date I gave a certain amount of money." That confession is looking only at your action, the formula, and has no anchor of assurance. Your assurance can only come from the Word of God.

I cannot count the number of people I have prayed with that when asked why they believe they will receive when I pray simply stare at me with no answer. When I ask, I am looking for their faith, their agreement with heaven. I want to hear them say, "I know I will receive because God has promised me in such and such book of the Bible and in such and such verse that it is mine." Chances are if they cannot give me a Scripture, they are not anchored and they really do not have a clue where their boat is going.

Remember, faith can only exist when you know the will of God. Why? Because faith can only exist when your heart is in agreement with the will of God. I believe that many people think they are in faith when they are not. Again, their minds may agree that the Word of God is true and good, but faith is there only when their hearts are fully persuaded. For many, their minds agree with the Word of God, but their hearts are not settled.

Here is a good illustration of what I am talking about, one which I believe will point out that many are not in faith when they think they are. What if I were to tell you that I had recently found out that the sky was not blue, as people said, but that the color blue as they called it was really the color yellow? In other words, I told you that we had been taught wrong all our lives about colors and that blue is not really blue but yellow. What would you do? Would you gasp in shock and quickly grab your cell phone and call your first grade teacher and yell at them, accusing them of messing up your life, teaching you all the colors wrong? I do not think so. There would be no emotional reaction of fear, no drama. You would simply know that I was an idiot, dismiss the comment as irrational, and go about your business. Why? Because you are fully persuaded that blue is blue!

Now, let's compare my example to our faith discussion. What if you were fully persuaded of what God said about healing, and a doctor told you that you were going to die of cancer? You would look at that doctor and think he was the idiot because you knew there was no way that could happen. Why? It's because you were fully persuaded of the healing provisions that Jesus paid for. Do you see it? Of course, many people pray, but upon examination, I find their prayers are not prayers of faith but of hope, with them unsure of the outcome. My friend, this is why it is so important that we build ourselves up with the Word of God. We need to know what God's will is so that we can be confident in what He says, and also so we can reject what is not His will. Let me give you an example from my own life which illustrates just how important it is to feed on what God says about life.

I was tired, as it had been a tough few weeks as a business

owner (this was before I pastored a church). My schedule had been packed with sales calls and, of course, the financial pressure of living on commissions. I was going to my dentist for a routine filling. Everything was normal until the dentist went to inject the Novocain. As he inserted the needle, there was a sudden jolt, and then my jaw instantly went numb, as opposed to it slowly numbing up. I was surprised, and I told the dentist what had happened. He said, "Oh, I guess I hit the nerve." I quickly asked him, "Is that normal?" He said these words, "Well, it usually heals up." What? Did I hear him correctly? "Doctor, what do you mean it usually heals up?" He said, "Well, about 80 percent to 85 percent of the time, it completely heals up with no permanent negative effect."

What? Suddenly fear rose up in me. Now what? Is it going to heal up? My mind was starting to be consumed with fearful thoughts. After my appointment, my face stayed numb, unlike a normal dentist's appointment where the numbness slowly wears off. I was heading to a client's appointment about an hour away from the dentist's appointment, so I had plenty of time to think about what had just happened. But all the way to that appointment, I was in agony, not from any pain but from the lack of peace and from the fear that was swirling through my mind.

On the way home from the appointment, later in the day, I stopped at a friend's house. My face was still numb, and I was looking for some reassurance from someone that this thing would heal up. Notice my mistake: I did not look to the Word of God but to a person who was not even a strong believer for my confidence. I told this person what had happened and was waiting for their, "That's no big deal, Gary; it

AT THAT POINT, I KNEW THAT MY ONLY HOPE WAS THE WORD OF GOD.

will heal up!" Instead, here is what I heard. "Oh, no! I had a friend who had that happen, and their face never healed. Their face has been paralyzed ever since." I could not believe what I was hearing! My mind was then in fear overdrive. I acted like I knew it would be okay and thanked him for his time.

In desperation, I stopped by another friend's home and asked the same question, and in shock, I heard the same reply, "Oh, no," they said, "I had a friend who had this happen, and their face never healed. Their face is still paralyzed today."

After this visit, I was undone. I knew that God heals (in my mind), but I just could not get rid of that fear. My heart was definitely not persuaded. That night, I was in agony! My mind was full of fear, and my face was still just as numb as it had been at the dentist's office. As I was trying to get to sleep, I began to feel a bit of pain under my right ear. Could it be? My dad had fought a battle with Bell's palsy a year or two earlier, and he had told me that it had started with some pain just under his ear. Bell's palsy occurs when the nerve that controls the facial muscles, which travels through a small hole in the bone just under the ear, becomes pinched by an infection or inflammation.

As I lay there trying to find sleep, all I could hear were these words going through my thoughts, "You are going to have Bell's palsy just like your dad." When I woke up in the morning, I had a full-blown case of Bell's palsy! Not only was my jaw numb, but also my entire face on the right side was numb, and I could not close my eyes or my mouth. I was a mess.

I went to a local doctor to confirm my suspicions. After the examination, he looked at me and said that I indeed had a full-blown case of Bell's palsy. I then said, "What happens next?" He said, "Well, in about 80 to 85 percent of the cases, it will heal up without permanent paralysis." "Did he say what I thought he just said?"

At that point, I knew that I was in trouble. I knew that the devil would not stop there, and I did not want to see what came next. I knew enough about spiritual warfare to realize I was heading in the wrong direction. Remember, this was years ago before I knew very much about these types of things. But I knew enough to realize that I had to tackle this thing spiritually if I was going to have any success at beating it. I also realized that this was a demonic setup to catch me off guard when I was tired and not anticipating any trouble.

I knew then that my only hope was the Word of God. In myself, I had absolutely no ability to stop the fear that was plaguing my mind. So I wrote out 3 x 5 cards with healing Scriptures on them and posted them all over my house. I repented before the Lord and began the process of developing faith in my heart. I knew that I had to sow the Word in my heart for faith to develop, so I would meditate on the Word of God throughout the day.

At first, nothing changed. My face stayed numb, and I constantly fought the spirit of fear. After about a week, with still nothing changing in my face, it happened!

Just like the process our Scripture in Mark 4:26-28 teaches, as I sowed the Word into my heart, faith began to be formed, first the blade, then the stalk, the head, and then the mature grain in the head.

Throughout this entire process, there was not agreement and thus no faith—yet. However, even though I did not see change or know how this process works, according to our Scripture in Mark 4, things were indeed changing.

The change I am talking about is not in the manifested natural realm yet, but the change is occurring in our hearts. If we hold on to the Word, the Word slowly changes our hearts' belief system from one of unbelief to agreement with heaven all by itself.

So in this case, I held on to the Word, knowing that it was my only answer. Suddenly, one day, as I was walking through my house with all those 3 x 5 cards with healing Scriptures on them posted everywhere, I just happened to glance at one that I had seen a hundred times. But this time when I looked at it, BAM! Suddenly, the anointing came on me, fear instantly left, and I KNEW that I was healed. Yes, my face was still numb. There was no change, but I knew I was healed. Within a couple of hours, my face was completely normal, with all the numbness gone. Praise God! The Word works!

Even though I had allowed my spiritual life to weaken due to my neglect and busyness, I eventually realized my mistake and repented from my foolishness. This was way back when I was first learning how faith really worked, and I did not have a lot of experience in this area. I look back on what I did, asking people of my future when in trouble instead of going straight to the Word of God, as foolish. Once I understood what was going on, I did turn to the Word of God with confidence. Unfortunately, most people are not confident in this process because they have never been taught about faith and how it comes. Since they are unaware of the process, when they are under pressure, they let go of the Word, thinking it does not work.

Understand Satan's counterattack.

Christine came to our church not knowing much about God. She was born again in one of our Sunday morning services, and her life was radically changed. In our church, we have a Kingdom orientation class. One of the areas we talk and teach about is the legal right to receive healing. Christine had been having trouble with her hearing for years. In fact, she had been wearing a hearing aid for 40 years and had already lost over 50 percent of her hearing. Her mother was deaf, and her brother was also suffering from this same issue with loss of hearing. When Christine heard that, as a believer, she had a legal right to be healed, she was so excited!

In the class, my wife, Drenda, laid her hands on her and prayed for her ears to be open, and instantly, pop, she could hear perfectly. Christine began screaming and crying and praising God. When Drenda and Christine came and told me the good news, I felt an urge to warn her about Satan's counterattack. I told Drenda to instruct Christine that if the symptoms started to come back for her to speak boldly to the issue and declare that she was healed and for Satan to back off. The next morning, the test came. Her hearing had reverted back to her inability to hear well. So, she did exactly what we said, "NO! Satan, I am not receiving this. I am healed, and I *was* healed, in the name of Jesus!" Pop! Her ears popped open, and they have stayed open ever since.

Remember that Satan will counterattack and try to retake territory. Don't let him do it. Stand on the Word of God!

In this appendix, I have taken some time to give you a basic understanding of what faith is, how it functions, how to know if you are in faith, and where to get faith. For the Kingdom of God to operate in your life, you have to know this. Remember, Jesus told the woman that received her healing in Matthew 9:20-22, *"Your faith has healed you."* And so shall it be for you: Your faith, your heart being fully convinced of what heaven says, and putting in the sickle will be your answer for any problem or need you may face in life.[14]

14. The teaching in the Faith Appendix was taken from my *Your Financial Revolution: The Power of Allegiance* book.

HOLY SPIRIT APPENDIX

THE BASICS: DON'T LEAVE HOME WITHOUT THIS

If you are going to lead a life full of Holy Spirit strategies and Holy Spirit led victories, first, you need to be born again and then, secondly, baptized in the Holy Spirit. Yes, they are two completely different works of the same Spirit. If this is something totally foreign to you, that's all right. I will walk you through it. But let me get right to the point, Jesus said it was so important to have the Baptism of the Holy Spirit that He said you shouldn't leave home without it! Again, I did not say that; Jesus did in Acts 1:4-5.

> *Do not leave Jerusalem, but wait for the gift my Father promised, which you have heard me speak about. For John baptized with water, but in a few days you will be <u>baptized with the Holy Spirit</u>.*
>
> —Acts 1:4b-5

> *But you will receive power when the Holy Spirit comes on you; and you will be my witnesses.*
>
> —Acts 1:8a

Notice Jesus said, "Don't leave home without this—this is essential!" Basically, He was saying, "You need this power to do the works of God, to be a witness of the Kingdom. Yet today, there are multitudes of Christians who have yet to hear of or experience the Baptism of the Holy Spirit, multitudes of Christians who have been raised in church but still have never heard of the need for the Baptism of the Holy Spirit. Or they were raised in church and were told that the baptism isn't for today, that miracles have passed away.

I was raised in a church like that and never heard of the Baptism of the Holy Spirit. I get so many emails from people all over the world who have yet to hear of this powerful truth as well. Many of the emails I receive question the validity of this gift for today, which is why I have taken the time to put on paper the truth concerning the Baptism of the Holy Spirit.

I believe the Bible is very clear concerning this area, and I want to let the Bible speak for itself. It will answer all of your questions. But, first, I want to give you some background on how I discovered the truth about the Baptism of the Holy Spirit.

When I was younger, I was hungry for God (still am, although I am older), and I attended a denominational church. We went through the normal religious routines on Sunday morning. Maybe you did too. I remember a couple of hymns followed by a silent moment of meditation. We always quoted the Lord's Prayer, and then the pastor gave a sermon, a closing hymn, and a benediction. Every service was laid out in the same way.

The people there were wonderful and, yes, they really loved God. But I never really saw the reality of the Gospel. I didn't see people's lives dramatically changed or people healed by the power of God. I guess I could say that I didn't see a lot of demonstration of the Kingdom of God.

So, there I was hungry for God, 18 years old, and running my dad's pizza shop. One night, a guy came into the pizza shop and invited me to a revival. It was being held at a small Methodist church in my town, and the guest speaker was an evangelist who spoke about Jesus doing the same things today as He did in the Bible.

Now, that caught my attention because I wanted to see that. A couple of my friends attended this church, so I decided to visit the revival. Although I didn't hear about the Baptism of the Holy Spirit that night, I was deeply touched by the presence of God in that service. My friends that were attending there encouraged me to come back on a Sunday, which I did. I fell in love with that church and made it my new church home.

A few weeks after the revival, I met a group of women who attended the church and also held a weekly Bible study. They were talking about something called the Baptism of the Holy Spirit, the gifts of the Spirit, and various other things I had never heard of before. I was so eager to hear about this power they spoke of that I asked them if I could come to their women's Bible study. Their Bible study was in the mornings, and since I worked at night in the pizza shop, I decided to attend.

When I got there, I found out that I was indeed the only guy there and the only 18-year-old as well, but that didn't matter to me. I went to the Bible study because I was hungry for God. I asked so many questions.

The ladies were so patient with me and took me through the Scriptures and showed me in my own Bible that the Baptism of the Holy Spirit is for today and that the power of God is available today just as it was when Jesus walked the earth. The best part was when they said it is for *all* believers—it's for anyone who asks.

After I had attended the Bible study for a couple of weeks, they told me that a national ministry called Women's Aglow was holding a citywide meeting. Women's Aglow was and still is an organization that teaches a lot about the Baptism of the Holy Spirit. These women were planning to attend, and they invited me to go with them. In those days, people from all denominations would gather to hear about and enjoy this baptism that, up until that point, was mainly talked about only in the Pentecostal churches. Those were the days many people call the Charismatic Renewal, where this teaching of the Holy Spirit crossed over all denominational lines.

When I attended the Women's Aglow meeting, I saw that hundreds of ladies had gathered. Again, I was in the minority as a man, but there was a presence of God in that room that was tangible.

I marveled as people were speaking of being healed, and I watched in amazement as some who were prayed for fell to the ground. This was something I had never seen before, and I was curious and a little confused by it. I found out that the people there called it being slain in the Spirit. Although in the natural it seemed a little strange to me, the people who experienced it seemed to get up elated and were obviously touched by God. Later, I found out from the ladies that our flesh can't contain the power of God and can sometimes be overwhelmed by what they called "the anointing."

They showed me where this happened in Jesus's own ministry. In John 18:4b-6 when the soldiers came for Jesus to arrest Him, Jesus asked,

"Who is it you want?" "Jesus of Nazareth," they replied. "I am he," Jesus said... When Jesus said, "I am he," they drew back and <u>fell to the ground</u>.

During worship, the ladies around me were all so excited, and I heard many people around me speaking and praising God in tongues. The whole experience was so new to me that for most of the meeting I just stood in awe. Although there were many aspects of the meeting that were a little strange to me, I could not deny the incredible and tangible presence of God. I was so excited to find the reality of the Gospel, the power of God, was still operating in the earth, just like in the Bible.

That day, the speaker asked anyone who wanted to receive this gift of the Holy Spirit to come forward for prayer at the end of the meeting. So, I went forward to have the ladies pray with me. As they prayed, I found myself overwhelmed as the presence of God got even stronger. As I yielded to His presence, I was amazed to hear myself actually begin to pray in the Holy Spirit and speak out words that I did not understand. I prayed in tongues for quite a while that night. I was so overwhelmed by the experience, I wanted to tell everyone I met about what had happened to me! But when I shared with my friends at church what I had experienced, they weren't so excited. They would usually say that tongues were of the devil or that it had passed away. They warned me to stay away from those Holy Rollers!

In those days, churches weren't open to the gifts of the Spirit, and the prevailing doctrine was that miracles had passed away with the apostles. But I understood then that God's power hadn't passed away at all!

Just before this Women's Aglow event took place, I had been

put in charge of the youth in that small Methodist church. There really wasn't that much required of me except that we would have a youth meeting every Sunday night in the church basement. We would usually play some games, have refreshments, and have a brief Bible study. I was really just a youth myself, but they saw that I had a zeal for the things of God and was willing to help out.

There were usually about 15 kids in the group, and after what happened to me that day at the Women's Aglow meeting, I wanted to tell them about this Baptism of the Holy Spirit I had experienced. I realized that, like me, most of them hadn't even heard of this experience, and I knew that they weren't going to hear about it during Sunday morning service at that particular church.

Before I tell you what happened next, I think I should give you a quick update on my mindset at the time. I didn't get the pastor's permission to talk about this with the youth. (I now realize that I should have.) I also didn't tell him what had happened to me either. I wasn't trying to walk in rebellion against my church, and I wasn't trying to go around my pastor. I was just excited. At that time, I really didn't understand the controversy over this topic, and I certainly didn't think the pastor would be against it.

The Sunday night after I received the Baptism of the Holy Spirit, I planned to tell the youth about what had happened to me and to show them some of the Scriptures that talked about it in the book of Acts. We were in the church basement just sitting on the floor in a circle when I shared my experience with them and went through some of the Scriptures verifying the experience.

This particular evening, the pastor came to the meeting and was sitting on my left as I shared. I thought nothing of my pastor being there. As my pastor, I thought he already knew everything I was going to share anyway.

So, I shared with them about the meeting I had gone to and about the things I saw. I didn't really go into much detail about speaking in tongues. Instead, I focused my attention on Acts 1:8 where it says we will receive *power* when the Holy Spirit comes upon us to be a witness for God. At the end of the meeting, I really didn't know how to end my lesson, so I just asked the kids to raise their hand if they wanted to receive the Baptism of the Holy Spirit.

I didn't know what to do at that point. I mean, I had never seen anyone minister to someone about the Baptism of the Holy Spirit except what I had seen at the Women's Aglow meeting. I think I might have known only two or three Scriptures referring to it at the time.

So, I just said, "If you would like to receive this free gift of the Holy Spirit, just raise your hand, and let's bow our heads and pray." That's really all I said. I didn't touch them or coach them on how to receive the Holy Spirit. We bowed our heads and prayed. Of course, we closed our eyes to pray like all "good" denominational Christians were taught.

As I sat there after I said "Amen," I began to hear some commotion among the kids. I opened my eyes and saw that some of the kids were crying, some were shaking, and seven kids had started speaking in tongues. As they started speaking in tongues, I saw the most unusual glow on their faces. They were lit up like lightbulbs! I was shocked!

My pastor, who had said nothing up until this point, quickly tapped me on the shoulder and asked if he could talk to me right away. We walked into the next room, and he looked me in the eye and said, "This is of the devil. You can't be the youth leader here anymore. We're not going to have this."

I thought, *How can you say it's of the devil? I mean look at these kids! They're glowing!* You could see the anointing physically on them. Of course, I didn't even know what the word anointing was back then. I just knew that they were glowing, and I hadn't touched them or told them how to act. It was very discouraging and confusing to me to have my pastor rebuke me like that, and I didn't know what to do.

The next Sunday, I made my way back to church, but instead of sitting up near the front of the church where I usually sat, I sat in the back. I knew I was kind of in the doghouse with my pastor because of the youth meeting, and I thought I had better lay low for a bit while I figured things out.

During the Sunday morning service, there was the usual silent moment of meditation. This was a very respectful and quiet moment of prayer in my church. Everyone's head was bowed, and there wasn't a sound in the church. You could hear a pin drop. It was at this very moment that I felt someone tap me on my shoulder. I was on the end of the pew, and apparently someone was standing up in the aisle and tapping me on my shoulder.

At first, I was shocked to think that someone was up walking during the very quiet and reserved moment of prayer. When I looked up, I was surprised to see one of the kids who had been in the youth meeting the week before. I also knew that he was one of the seven that had received the Baptism of the Holy Spirit that night. He looked at me and said, "Let's go!" I thought, *Let's go? Let's go where?*

Amazingly, he was glowing just like he was the night he had received the Holy Spirit, and I knew God was doing something. But I wasn't sure this was the time or place to do anything since I was already in trouble with the pastor. I also knew that we couldn't just do anything we wanted to in Sunday morning church. That's when he said, "I'm going to go pray for my mom."

Then, I was beginning to understand what was going on. I knew his mother. She was a small, thin woman and had been sick for a very long time. She had five vertebrae in her back that had deteriorated, and the doctor's only hope was to fuse them together. This surgery was very serious, and my friend was her only child. Of course he was concerned for his mother.

After receiving the Baptism of the Holy Spirit, he felt sure that Jesus would heal his mother. So, when he said, "Let's go," I thought he was going to go up there and lay his hands on his mom and pray for her quietly. But that's not what he did. He went up to his mother, picked her up right off the pew, and carried her to the front of the church.

He sat her down and began to pray for her as loud as he could in tongues. Now remember, this all took place during the "silent" moment of meditation, which wasn't so silent anymore. I was shocked! Then he turned to me and said, "You explain what's going on."

Then I understood why he had me come along. He figured I was the one who had told him about the Baptism of the Holy Spirit, so he figured that I could tell the congregation about it after they heard him praying in tongues for his mother.

So, there I was standing in front of the congregation as his spokesman, and there he was praying for his mom in tongues. I really didn't know what to say, especially since my pastor sat there glaring at me. I simply told the congregation that his mother had been sick and that he was praying for her in tongues, which was in the Bible. But you know what? She was instantly healed that morning in church!

That was the faith of a son who really didn't care what anyone else thought about him praying. He was convinced that the Holy Spirit was alive and well and could heal his mother.

Even though she was instantly healed, the church didn't receive it. In fact, many of them came to me afterwards and said, "Well, I didn't mind him praying for his mom, but those tongues, we can't handle that tongues thing." Well, I can guarantee that the devil hates the tongues thing as well, and I hope to help you understand why he hates tongues before this book is over.

Maybe you grew up in a church where tongues and the gifts of the Spirit weren't practiced. Or maybe you grew up being taught that tongues were not for today or had passed away. These questions aren't hard to answer. The Bible is very clear on this subject. So, let's take a good look at the Word and find out the truth on the Baptism of the Holy Spirit. Let's go back to the verses we read at the beginning of this chapter.

> *Do not leave Jerusalem, but wait for the gift my Father promised, which you have heard me speak about. For John baptized with water, but in a few days you will be baptized with the Holy Spirit.*
> —Acts 1:4b-5

There are several important points we can see in this verse:

1. The Baptism of the Holy Spirit is different than being baptized in water.

2. Jesus said it was extremely important. In fact, He made it clear that you wouldn't be able to do anything without it.

Remember, Jesus had just told the disciples to go and preach the Gospel to every nation, but they wouldn't be able to demonstrate or verify the Kingdom of heaven without this baptism. So, he said, "Stay put until you receive this empowering."

> *But you will receive power when the Holy Spirit comes on you; and you will be my witnesses in Jerusalem, and in all Judea and Samaria, and to the ends of the earth.*
> —Acts 1:8

Power! The Greek word for power here is *dunamis* and is where we get our word for dynamite.[15] [16] So we see that God's power comes on us to do His works. Earlier in Jesus's ministry, He had mentioned that the power, or that anointing He was operating under, was from His Father.

> *The words I say to you I do not speak on my own authority. Rather, it is the Father, living in me, who is doing his work.*
> —John 14:10b

> *I tell you the truth, the Son can do nothing by himself.*
> —John 5:19b (NLT)

You see, Jesus needed that empowerment of the Spirit of God Himself. The word *anointing* means to "apply to." Jesus received that anointing at the River Jordan from His Father when the Holy Spirit came on Him in the form of a dove.

15. *The American Heritage® Dictionary of the English Language, Fifth Edition.* Copyright ©2022 by HarperCollins Publishers. All rights reserved.
16. James Strong, *Strong's Exhaustive Concordance of the Bible*, Hendrickson Publishers.

It was only after Jesus received that anointing that He was able to do the works of the Kingdom. If *Jesus* needed it, we need it too! That power will testify (or give witness) through demonstration that God is real to those who don't know Him.

The Bible also says that you will receive power when the Holy Spirit COMES ON YOU, not when He comes *in* you as when you're born again.

Many are confused when we talk about the Baptism of the Holy Spirit, thinking that they've already received the Holy Spirit when they accepted Christ. And the truth is they *did* receive the Holy Spirit when they received Christ. The Holy Spirit made their spirits alive to God and one with God.

We are alive to God by the power of the Holy Spirit on the inside of us when we're born again. But notice that Acts 1:8 says when the Holy Spirit comes <u>on</u> you. This is an important fact that we'll cover later on in this appendix: being born again and being anointed or baptized by the Holy Spirit are two different events. We can get a better understanding of this if we look at John 20:21-22.

> *Again Jesus said, "Peace be with you! As the Father has sent me, I am sending you." And with that he breathed on them and said, "Receive the Holy Spirit."*

We see Jesus here after His resurrection as He greets His disciples and breathes on them and tells them to receive the Holy Spirit. This is the moment that they are born again and their spirits come alive to God on the inside. Yet Jesus tells them to wait for the Baptism of the Holy Spirit, which will <u>come upon</u> them on a later day.

If they had received all of the Holy Spirit when Jesus breathed on them, why would He tell them to wait in Jerusalem until they received the Holy Spirit that was promised to come upon them? Again, these are two different events and two different functions, but the same Spirit. Also, as I said, I want to point out that Jesus had to be baptized by the Holy Spirit to enter into and be effective in His ministry as well. Before Jesus was baptized in the Holy Spirit, there is no record of Him doing one single miracle. Did Jesus multiply bread at the supper table when He was growing up? Did He do miracles when He was a baby? Did He multiply His baby food when it ran out because He was still hungry? No! He didn't. Why didn't He? The simple and honest answer is: He *couldn't*.

It wasn't until *after* He received the Holy Spirit at the River Jordan that He began to do miracles. You see, Jesus came as a man. He didn't come as the Son of God in His power and glory. As a man, He was limited as any man is limited. He couldn't heal or do any miracles, just as you and I can't do any miracles in and of ourselves either.

However, unlike us, Jesus's spirit was not dead to God when He was born as a baby. His spirit was always alive to God; He didn't need to be born again as we do. Although His spirit was alive to God as a Son, He still needed to be baptized by the Holy Spirit before He could begin His ministry, just as we do.

> *As soon as Jesus was baptized, he went up out of the water. At that moment heaven was opened, and he saw the Spirit of God descending like a dove and alighting on him. And a voice from heaven said, "This is my Son, whom I love; with him I am well pleased.*
>
> —Matthew 3:16-17

Remember, we think of Jesus as King of kings and the Lord of lords, but this isn't the position from which He ministered. It was only after the Holy Spirit came upon Him at the River Jordan that the miracles begin.

Your ministry (because *every* believer is called to do the works of Jesus) can't begin until you are baptized with the Holy Spirit—you need the power of the Holy Spirit to get things done. And you need the ability to pray in the Spirit to know how to do them, as we will discuss later.

Of course, you can offer the born-again experience by telling others what the Bible says about salvation. A lot of Christians who aren't baptized in the Holy Spirit are effective in sharing the Good News of the Gospel, but they don't have the power to demonstrate the Kingdom as Jesus did. This causes a lot of weak preaching.

When Jesus confronted the Pharisees concerning their unbelief, He made reference to the miracles He was doing. He said,

> *"Believe that I live as one with my Father and that my Father lives as one in me—or <u>at least</u>, believe because of the mighty miracles I have done."*
> —John 14:11 (TPT)

Jesus was basically saying that this demonstration of the Kingdom puts a stop to all argument; the issue is settled. Now, of course, every believer has full legal rights to everything Jesus paid for, including healing. Every believer can receive every promise of God by faith (agreement with heaven), and they do not need the Baptism of the Holy Spirit to receive from God.

But for that power to flow from you to others, and for you to flow in the gifts of the Spirit and to enjoy the benefit of walking in heavenly mysteries through praying in tongues, you must have the power of that anointing! I realize that you may not understand what I mean when I say praying in tongues. Don't let it scare you; I will fully explain it.

SCRIPTURAL EVIDENCE

One of the best ways to gain an understanding of the Baptism of the Holy Spirit is to follow those who received it on the Day of Pentecost as recorded in the book of Acts. As we examine each Scripture, your faith and confidence will grow that this baptism is for you as well.

> When the day of Pentecost came, they were all together in one place. Suddenly a sound like the blowing of a violent wind came from heaven and filled the whole house where they were sitting. They saw what seemed to be tongues of fire that separated and came to rest on each of them. All of them were filled with the Holy Spirit and began to speak in other tongues as the Spirit enabled them.
>
> Now there were staying in Jerusalem God-fearing Jews from every nation under heaven. When they heard this sound, a crowd came together in bewilderment, because each one heard them speaking in his own language.
>
> Utterly amazed, they asked: "Are not all these men who are speaking Galileans? Then how is it that each of us hears them in his own native language? Parthians, Medes and Elamites; residents of Mesopotamia, Judea and Cappadocia, Pontus and Asia, Phrygia and Pamphylia, Egypt and the parts of Libya

near Cyrene; visitors from Rome (both Jews and converts to
Judaism); Cretans and Arabs—we hear them declaring the
wonders of God in our own tongues!"

Amazed and perplexed, they asked one another, "What does
this mean?" Some, however, made fun of them and said, "They
have had too much wine."

—Acts 2:1-13

The first thing I want you to see is that the Bible says **all of
them** were filled with the Holy Spirit! Secondly, they *all* spoke in
tongues. Perhaps you've heard people describe the Day of Pentecost and explain why they all spoke in tongues. Some insist that it
was a one-time experience for the church because the people were
gathered there from many nations and so, consequently, tongues
were needed to preach the Gospel to all the people of different
languages.

But if you look at the Scripture, you'll see it says the 120 who
were in the upper room were speaking of the wonderful works of
God. They weren't preaching the Gospel; they were just praising
God.

"We hear them declaring the wonders of God in our own
tongues!" Amazed and perplexed, they asked one another,
"What does this mean?"

—Acts 2:11b-12

The people standing around hearing them praising God in
their own native languages were all amazed and perplexed. Peter
then stood up and preached the message of salvation, and 3,000
were added to the church that day. Now, if the disciples had been

preaching in tongues, Peter wouldn't have had to stand up and preach. But until Peter stood to preach, they did not know what they were hearing meant. Tongues weren't used to preach the Gospel then, and they're not used to preach the Gospel now. We will cover the benefit of tongues to the believer in this appendix, but for now, I am just addressing a common argument I have heard.

Again, I want to make the point that the Bible says they *all* received and they *all* spoke in tongues. Now if the Bible leaves us right there, we might have some doubt that speaking in tongues is for the entire church. But the Bible doesn't do that. Instead, we find this phenomenon continues and happens for *every single person* who receives the Baptism of the Holy Spirit after the Day of Pentecost.

Let me tell you about one of the men who was present on the Day of Pentecost—his name was Phillip.

> *Those who had been scattered preached the word wherever they went. Phillip went down to a city in Samaria and proclaimed the Messiah there. When the crowds heard Phillip and saw the signs he performed they all paid close attention to what he said.*
>
> —Acts 8:4-6

Here we see Philip demonstrating the Kingdom and the people listening. That's how it's supposed to be today! When people *see* the signs, when they *see* the *evidence* of the Kingdom, they're going to pay close attention to what you say.

> *Many evil spirits were cast out, screaming as they left their*

victims. And many who had been paralyzed or lame were also
healed. So there was great joy in that city.

—Acts 8:7-8 (NLT)

Notice that Phillip was walking in the power that he had just received while in Jerusalem. Signs followed him, as the power of God was evident to all. He had received that *dunamis* (Greek word for *power*, as I mentioned before); he was now able to be a witness of the Kingdom of God.

> *When the apostles in Jerusalem heard that Samaria had*
> *accepted the word of God, they sent Peter and John to Samaria.*
> *When they arrived, they prayed for the new believers that they*
> *might receive the Holy Spirit, because the Holy Spirit had not*
> *yet <u>come on</u> any of them; they had simply been baptized into the*
> *name of the Lord Jesus. Then Peter and John placed their hands*
> *on them, and they received the Holy Spirit.*
>
> —Acts 8:14-17

When the apostles in Jerusalem heard that Samaria had accepted the Word of God, they sent Peter and John to them. When they arrived, they prayed for them that they might receive the Holy Spirit because the Holy Spirit had <u>not yet come on</u> any of them. Yet the Bible just said that demons left, people were healed, mighty works of God had just occurred, and the people believed in Jesus and were baptized in water. But it also says that the Holy Spirit had not <u>COME ON</u> any of them yet!

You see, Phillip preached salvation and they accepted it and received it, but they hadn't received the Holy Spirit's baptism yet. They were born again, but look at the wording: The Holy Spirit had not yet "COME ON ANY OF THEM." There's that difference again—the Holy Spirit *in* us (being born again) and the Holy Spirit coming *upon* us with that endowment of power.

The Bible doesn't say why Phillip hadn't preached to them about the Baptism of the Holy Spirit. It's possible that he left Jerusalem immediately after being baptized with the Holy Spirit himself and at that time didn't know it was for everyone. Whatever the reason, it was evident that the people had believed the Gospel and been water baptized, so they were born again. But notice how important it was to the apostles that the people in Samaria receive the Baptism of the Holy Spirit as they had—immediately.

The first thought they had wasn't to tell them how to dress. They didn't say, "Let's tell them how to dress righteously or when to hold church." They weren't concerned with rules of doctrine. What was the first thing they were concerned about? The Baptism of the Holy Spirit! So they made the effort to head up there immediately and tell these guys all about the Baptism in the Holy Spirit.

Then Peter and John placed their hands on them, and they received the Holy Spirit. Right then and there they received the Holy Spirit. What was the evidence? I believe it was just like everyone else's: praying in tongues.

> *When Simon saw that the Spirit was given at the laying on of the apostles' hands, he offered them money and said, "Give me also this ability so that everyone on whom I lay my hands may receive the Holy Spirit."*
>
> *Peter answered: "May your money perish with you, because you thought you could buy the gift of God with money! You have no part or share in this ministry, because your heart is not right before God. Repent of this wickedness and pray to the Lord in*

the hope that he may forgive you for having such a thought in your heart.

Then Simon answered, "Pray to the Lord for me so that nothing you have said may happen to me."

—Acts 8:18-24

When Simon saw that the Spirit was given with the laying on of hands, he offered the apostles money to give him that kind of power. Simon must have seen something, some evidence that something happened when they received the Holy Spirit. He wanted that power. Now, it doesn't say they spoke in tongues right there, but something happened visibly that they could see. Simon saw something that was powerful, and he wanted to have the ability to give that to people. I believe his comments show that they received that baptism just like everyone else did and began speaking in tongues. Again, I want to point out just how important the church in Jerusalem viewed the Baptism of the Holy Spirit as—it was vital!

When Paul's conversion took place on the road to Damascus, a man named Ananias was sent to Paul to pray for him.

Ananias said, "Brother Saul, the Lord—Jesus, who appeared to you on the road as you were coming here—has sent me so that you may see again and be filled with the Holy Spirit."

—Acts 9:17b

The Bible doesn't say that Paul spoke in tongues when he received the Baptism of the Holy Spirit, but we know that he did speak in tongues, and I believe he received it just like everyone else did. You may ask why I would believe that. That's easy. It's because of what Paul himself wrote in 1 Corinthians 14:18.

"I thank God that I speak in tongues more than all of you" (1 Corinthians 14:18).

So, we can come to the conclusion that Paul spoke in tongues when he was baptized in the Holy Spirit. As you read through the chapters of Acts, you'll discover that this baptism continued day after day throughout the church. It didn't just happen on the Day of Pentecost.

Later, in Acts 10, Peter is sent to Cornelius's home, a Gentile, and is led to preach the Gospel to a large group of people inside. Remember, this was highly unusual for Peter, who was a Jew, to go to a Gentile's home. He went only because he was led there by a vision from the Holy Spirit.

> *While Peter was still speaking these words, the Holy Spirit came on all who heard the message. The circumcised believers who had come with Peter were astonished that the gift of the Holy Spirit had been poured out even on the Gentiles. For they heard them speaking in tongues and praising God.*
>
> *Then Peter said, "Surely no one can stand in the way of people being baptized with water? They have received the Holy Spirit just as we have." So he ordered that they be baptized in the name of Jesus Christ. Then they asked Peter to stay with them for a few days.*
>
> —Acts 10:44-48

While Peter was preaching the Gospel of Christ at this Gentile's home, the Holy Spirit came on all who heard the message. You can't see the Spirit of God, so how did they know the Holy

Spirit came on them? The text says that the circumcised believers who had come with Peter were astonished that the gift of the Holy Spirit had been poured out even on the Gentiles, <u>for they heard them speaking in tongues and praising God</u>.

So, what was the evidence that the Holy Spirit was there? Peter had to recognize what was evident to him, that God had accepted these people. The fact that he saw them speaking in tongues when he had never even ministered to them anything about the Baptism of the Holy Spirit was all the evidence he needed. Peter *knew* they had received because they received the Holy Spirit just like he had—and they were praying in tongues.

You're going to find a huge difference between what the modern-day church thinks is important and what the church in biblical times thought was important. One of my favorite Scriptures that so clearly points out that everyone should be baptized in the Holy Spirit, and verifies without question that it's a work of the Holy Spirit apart from being born again, is in Acts 19:1-2.

> *While Apollos was at Corinth, Paul took the road through the interior and arrived at Ephesus. There he found some disciples and asked them, "Did you receive the Holy Spirit when you believed?" They answered, "No, we have not even heard that there is a Holy Spirit."*
>
> —Acts 19:1-2

When Paul entered the town of Ephesus, he found some disciples and he asked them, "Did you receive the Holy Spirit when you believed?" This was the first concern Paul had when he came across these believers.

Paul realized that being born again was distinctly different from being baptized with the Holy Spirit with the evidence of speaking in tongues.

Why would this be the very first thing Paul said to them? Because it was the same thing that Jesus said in Acts 1:4! He basically said, "Don't leave town without it!" What did the apostles do in Jerusalem when they found out that the people in Samaria had heard the Word? They said, "Boys, you get up there right now. We've got to make sure that this is set right. Get up there and make sure they have the Baptism of the Holy Spirit." When Paul, going through Ephesus, found some disciples, the first thing he asked them was, "Have you received the Holy Spirit since you've believed?"

When they answered, "No, we have not even heard that there is a Holy Spirit," Paul asked them what baptism they had received. They answered, "John's baptism." Paul said John's baptism was a baptism of repentance and told the people to believe in the One coming after him. That is, believe in Jesus.

On hearing this, they were baptized into the name of the Lord Jesus (water baptized). Afterward, when Paul placed his hands on them, the Holy Spirit came on them, and they spoke in tongues. Notice when Paul asked the question, he assumed they were believers in Jesus. That's why he asked, "Have you received the Holy Spirit since you believed?" He understood the Baptism of the Holy Spirit was distinctly different from being born again.

NOW, I BELIEVE THIS IS A CONTROVERSIAL TOPIC IN MANY CHURCHES, NOT BECAUSE IT'S NOT IN THE BIBLE BUT BECAUSE THE DEVIL HATES IT SO MUCH.

Now, I believe this is a controversial topic in many churches, not because it's not in the Bible but because the devil hates it so much.

Because if this is the power, if this is the doorway to the ability to change lives and to be a witness to the world, then you would be coming against the god of this world, and we know what his opinion of that would be. The Baptism of the Holy Spirit gives us a reservoir of power, God's power, to do the works of Jesus so that God is glorified!

DO ALL PRAY IN TONGUES?

Maybe you've heard someone say they don't speak in tongues and they don't believe that everyone can or should. They then quote 1 Corinthians 12:27-30 as the reason they believe that. They will point out that Paul himself said that everyone doesn't speak in tongues. Well, let's take a look at the text and see if that's really what Paul is saying.

> *Now you are the body of Christ, and members in particular. And some indeed God has appointed <u>in the church,</u> first apostles, secondly prophets, third teachers, then miracles, then gifts of healing, helping, administrating, various kinds of tongues. Are all apostles? Are all prophets? Are all teachers? Do all work miracles? Do all have gifts of healing? <u>Do all speak in tongues</u>? Do all interpret?*
>
> —1 Corinthians 12:27-30 (BSB)

In this letter, Paul is telling the church in Corinth how to operate in an orderly manner so that all may be ministered to in their church gatherings. At that time, they were all trying to outdo each other with their spiritual gifts and their favorite preachers. Paul was instructing them how to operate as a body in unity and in love. Now, let's take a closer look at 1 Corinthians 12:27-28 (BSB):

> *Now you are the body of Christ, and members in particular. And some indeed God has appointed <u>in the church</u> [I recommend you underline that phrase], first apostles, secondly prophets, third teachers, then miracles, then gifts of healing, helping, administrating, various kinds of tongues.*

Paul goes on there, but I'll stop because I want to talk a bit about that phrase, "in the church." He's talking about the actual church gathering. We can verify that over in 1 Corinthians 14:18-19 where Paul uses that same phrase:

> *I thank God that I speak in tongues more than all of you. But <u>IN THE CHURCH</u> I would rather speak five intelligible words to instruct others than ten thousand words in a tongue.*
> —1 Corinthians 14:18-19

Paul says, "I thank God that I speak in tongues more than all of you, "**but in the church**...." There's that phrase again, and this time it's clear that Paul is talking about the actual church gathering and not the universal body of Christ. We would all agree that Paul is part of the entire body of Christ, the "church." Of course he is. And he says that he's glad that he speaks in tongues more than all of the believers in Corinth. He said this because the church there was gloating in their new ability to speak in tongues, and they were out of order and causing confusion.

He is basically saying, "Hey guys, I speak in tongues more than all of you, but there is a way to carry this out 'in the church' that is done in order and doesn't cause confusion." He goes on to say that, in the church (the gathering of believers), he would rather speak with the understanding (in their common language) so that others may be edified.

In the church service itself, some people will operate in the gift of tongues and interpretation, as recorded in 1 Corinthians 12, but all will not or should not operate in that gift for the purpose of edifying the whole body. Paul even says to limit how many people should speak out in tongues and interpretation in a service to three people at the most.

"If anyone speaks in a tongue—two or at the most three—should speak, one at a time, and someone must interpret" (1 Corinthians 14:27).

So when Paul is saying all do not speak in tongues, he is referring to, "in the church," or the church gathering.

You need to understand that every believer will have the ability to pray in tongues, but not everyone will have that unction to step out into the gift of tongues and interpretation in a church service. If you do have that unction to step out in that gift in a service, the Bible says that you should pray that you may interpret.

"Anyone who speaks in a tongue should pray that they may interpret what they say" (1 Corinthians 14:13b).

I believe that the person speaking out in tongues is the most likely candidate to interpret in the service because the message is already flowing through them.

Why should you pray in tongues? The devil hates believers

who know how to pray in the Spirit (in tongues), and I want to be sure you understand why.

When Paul said that he was glad that he prayed in tongues more than anyone else, there must be a reason he felt that way. Paul made a comment in 1 Corinthians 14 that we need to read.

"*Anyone who speaks in a tongue* **edifies** *themselves, but the one who prophesies* **edifies** *the church*" (1 Corinthians 14:4).

Let's dig a little deeper. What does it mean to be edified? The word edify means "to instruct or benefit, especially morally or spiritually; to uplift." [17]

You would have to agree that there are many times when you need instruction to know which way to go, to understand a situation, or to make the right decision. This is what praying in tongues can help you with: to edify you or to bring instruction to your life. Paul makes this point clear in Romans 8:26-27:

> In the same way the Spirit helps us in <u>our weakness</u>. We do not know what we should pray for, but the Spirit himself intercedes for us with groans that are not expressed in words. And he who searches our hearts knows what the mind of the Spirit is, because the Spirit intercedes for the saints, according to God's will.
>
> —Romans 8:26-27 (EHV)

Paul tells us that we have a problem and a weakness: "We do not know what we should pray for." You may ask, "Why is this a

17. https://www.dictionary.com/edify

weakness?" We can understand why this is a weakness by reading
1 John 5:14-15.

> *This is the confidence we have in approaching God; that if*
> *we ask anything according to his will, he hears us. And if we*
> *know that he hears us—whatever we ask—we know we have*
> *what we asked of him.*

Without knowing or being confident of the will of God, we
cannot operate in faith (being in agreement with God), and if we
cannot operate in faith, then we are surely in a weak state because
we will not be able to tap into the grace or the power of God
without faith being present. So, Paul says that not knowing how
to pray is a weak condition that praying in tongues can help. Let's
read our text one more time.

> *In the same way the Spirit helps us in our weakness. <u>We do</u>*
> <u>*not know what we should pray for*</u>*.*
> —Romans 8:26a (EHV)

Our weakness is that we don't know how to pray! The Bible
doesn't tell us who to marry, where to live, or what job to take.
Without knowing the will of God, we can't know and believe that
we receive from God when we pray. Again, this is a huge weakness! We have no confidence in God when we don't know what
His will is. But there is a way that we can discern the will of God
in every situation in life. There's a way that we can be sure of God's
will so we can operate in faith and in confidence.

That's what Paul is talking about. This edification he is talking
about means having access to this kind of knowledge—the knowl-

edge that comes by the Spirit of God. And we tap into hearing the Spirit by praying in the Spirit, or in tongues. If we follow Paul's advice further in Romans 8:26b-27 (EHV), we read the following:

> *But the Spirit himself intercedes for us with groans that are not expressed in words. And he who searches our hearts knows what the mind of the Spirit is, because the Spirit intercedes for the saints in accordance with God's will.*

Now, Paul is not saying that we groan when we pray in the Spirit but, rather, Paul is referencing the preceding verses.

> *We know that the whole creation has been <u>groaning as in the pains of childbirth</u> right up to the present time. Not only so, but we ourselves, who have the firstfruits of the Spirit, <u>groan inwardly</u> as we wait eagerly for our adoption to sonship, the redemption of our bodies. For in this hope we were saved. But hope that is seen is no hope at all. Who hopes for what he already has? But if we hope for what we do not yet have, we wait for it patiently.*
>
> <u>*In the same way, the Spirit helps us in our weakness.*</u> *We do not know what we ought to pray for, but the Spirit himself intercedes for us with groans that words cannot express. And he who searches our hearts knows the mind of the Spirit, because the Spirit intercedes for the saints in accordance with God's will.*
>
> —Romans 8:22-27

Paul is using the word groan here as an illustration or an analogy of what is happening on the inside of us. We groan inwardly, like a woman giving birth. That is, we are giving birth to something from the Spirit of God within us, receiving something new, something that has never existed before; or you could say something not of ourselves. So we "birth" the knowledge of what we don't know, something new, out of our own spirits through the process of praying in the Spirit. The Bible tells us that God's Spirit prays the perfect will of God for any situation through our own spirits. It says that God Himself prays for us, through our own human spirits, with groans that can't be uttered (articulated in understood speech).

So, what we discover here is that the Holy Spirit is going to intercede for us with groans (birthing) using inarticulate words, words we do not understand (or tongues). And he who searches our hearts knows the mind of the Spirit because the Spirit (God's Spirit) intercedes for the saints in accordance with God's perfect will. The Spirit of God prays the perfect will of God for each situation <u>through your own spirit when you pray in tongues</u>.

So, we're in a weak place when we don't know the will of God. Faith can't be released until we know the will of God. Paul is saying that if we will pray in the Spirit, God's own Spirit will pray through us His perfect will for our lives in any situation.

As God's Spirit prays through us in tongues, how then do we become edified since we don't know what we're saying? The answer is found in another letter that Paul wrote.

> *What no eye has seen, what no ear has heard, and what no human mind has conceived—the things God has prepared for those who love him—these are the things God has revealed to us by his Spirit.*
>
> *The Spirit searches all things, even the deep things of God.*

For who knows a person's thoughts except their own spirit within them?

In the same way no one knows the thoughts of God except the Spirit of God. We have not received the spirit of the world but the Spirit who is from God, that we may understand what God has freely given us. This is what we speak, not in words taught us by human wisdom but in words taught by the Spirit, expressing spiritual truths in spiritual words.

—1 Corinthians 2:9b-13

First of all, Paul is saying that we have access to the things we have never heard, seen, or thought, just as I've been sharing with you. But he goes on and tells us how this works:

For who among men knows a person's thoughts except their own spirit within them? In the same way no one knows the thoughts of God except the Spirit of God.

—1 Corinthians 2:11

Before I cover this aspect of the Scripture, we need to first have a basic lesson in our makeup. According to 1 Thessalonians 5:23, we are three parts: spirit, soul, and body.

May God himself, the God of peace, sanctify you through and through. May your whole spirit, soul and body be kept blameless at the coming of our Lord Jesus Christ.

—1 Thessalonians 5:23

Our spirit is the God part of us; our soul is our mind, will, and emotions; and our body is our body. Paul is saying that our soul (mind, will, and emotions) and spirit are so closely connected that our spirit knows what our thoughts are.

The reverse is true as well. Our minds can pick up thoughts from our spirits. Paul says that God's Spirit knows God's thoughts and that we have received God's Spirit so that we <u>may know</u> what God has freely given us.

> *What we have received is not the spirit of the world, but the Spirit who is from God, so that we may understand what God has freely given us. This is what we speak, not in words taught us by human wisdom but in words taught by the Spirit, expressing spiritual realities with Spirit-taught words.*
>
> —1 Corinthians 2:12-13

Paul goes on to say that this unknown knowledge, knowledge that we did not know but is revealed to us by the Spirit of God, is what we speak with words that are taught to us by the Spirit, not words that we would speak in our natural understanding or language but spiritual words. We know that Paul is talking about praying in tongues when he says we pray with spiritual words because he used that same definition to describe speaking in tongues in 1 Corinthians 14:14-15:

> *For if I pray in a tongue, my spirit prays, but my mind is unfruitful. So what shall I do? I will pray with my spirit, but I will also pray with my understanding; I will sing with my spirit, but I will also sing with my understanding.*

Paul is using the phrase "pray in the spirit" as it refers to speaking in tongues. We can assume that Paul is referring to this same speaking in tongues when he says that we speak with words taught to us by the Spirit.

> *For anyone who speaks in a tongue does not speak to people but to God. Indeed, no one understands them; <u>they utter mysteries</u> by the Spirit.*
> —1 Corinthians 14:2

Again, Paul speaks of our spirit as having the ability to speak out things that we have never seen, heard, or had knowledge of, or as Paul says, "mysteries." Also notice in this verse that Paul says we are praying out mysteries <u>with our own spirit</u>, not God's Spirit. How does something we didn't know get into our spirit? That one is easy! By God's Spirit, who is now one with our spirit.

THE BAPTISM OF THE HOLY SPIRIT IS GOD'S SECRET WEAPON! HE CAN DOWNLOAD HIS WILL INTO THE EARTH WITHOUT THE DEVIL KNOWING WHAT IS GOING ON.

> *For who knows a person's thoughts except their own spirit within them? In the same way no one knows the thoughts of God except the Spirit of God.*
> —1 Corinthians 2:11

When our spirit picks up on the thoughts of God, our mind also picks up on these thoughts. When our minds pick up on the thoughts of God, we call this "revelation," being "enlightened," or, as Paul says, being "edified." Now you know why Paul said he was glad that he prayed in tongues more than anyone else; he received the benefit of knowing the will of God in every situation.

This is what Paul is referring to in 1 Corinthians 2:15-16.

> *But he who is spiritual judges all things, yet he himself is rightly judged by no one. For who has known the mind of the Lord that he may instruct him? But we have the mind of Christ.*
> —1 Corinthians 2:15-16 (NKJV)

We are not limited to simple human judgment, but we can make judgments about all things with God's help. This is great news! We have the ability, by praying in the Spirit (tongues), to receive mysteries, things we did not know; and by that knowledge, we are able to make right judgments or decisions about all things! The Baptism of the Holy Spirit is God's secret weapon! He can download His will into the earth without the devil knowing what is going on. In fact, praying in the Spirit is listed as part of our spiritual armor in Ephesians 6:18a:

> *And pray in the spirit on all occasions with all kinds of prayers and requests.*

Praying in the Spirit allows us to pick up on strategies that will allow us to sidestep the enemy, or to advance with unique and unusual tactics.

The implied benefit is that we can make right decisions in life by tapping into the mind of Christ. I think you would have to agree that this is vital! I have found it to be so!

As an example, I can remember having to make a huge decision in regard to my business. A sales rep I worked with, who represented one of my vendors, was threatening to take my company to court because I would not follow him to a new company. He wanted me to keep doing business with him as he left the vendor that I always did business with. I liked my sales rep, but I felt my loyalty was with the company he worked for, not with him. However, the company that he worked for had, in fact, told him that all his clients could transfer with him to his new company. So I would not be doing anything wrong to go with him, but yet I did not feel good about being forced to go with him. His current company had always been fair to me.

He was threatening to sue me because a few months earlier he had mentioned going with a new company and had asked me if I would go with him. Without really thinking about it, I had said I would. He said he was counting on my business when he made the decision to change companies. But then as he actually approached the date he was leaving, I had an uneasy feeling about it. So I prayed in the Spirit for a couple of days. But I still could not hear the answer that I needed.

Drenda and I often take our kids to a great amusement park that is a couple of hours away called Cedar Point. It is actually the biggest roller coaster park in the United States, and we usually go there a couple of times a year. It was a Friday night, and I had to have the answer on Monday morning as to what to do. I decided that it would be good to just get my mind on something else for a bit and decided to take Drenda up to the amusement park for the evening. As I was standing in line, not even thinking about that decision I had to make by Monday morning, all of a sudden, I knew exactly what to do. It was as clear as day. The Holy Spirit spoke to me, and I stayed with the parent company. The sales rep's new company folded up in a matter of a few months.

So, here is a major key to success—pray! And pray in the Spirit often so that all will go well with you and you will make right decisions, as well as pick up on the mysteries of strategy that you need to win.

"Pray continually" (1 Thessalonians 5:17).[18]

18. The teaching in the Holy Spirit Appendix was taken from my *Your Financial Revolution: The Power of Strategy* book.

ABOUT THE
AUTHOR

Gary Keesee is a television host, author, international speaker, financial expert, successful entrepreneur, and pastor who has made it his mission to help people win in life, especially in the areas of faith, family, and finances.

After years of living in poverty, Gary and his wife, Drenda, discovered the principles of the Kingdom of God, and their lives were drastically changed. Together, under the direction of the Holy Spirit, they created several successful businesses and paid off all of their debt. Now, they spend their time declaring the Good News of the Kingdom of God around the world through Faith Life Now, their organization that exists to motivate, educate, and inspire people from all walks of life and backgrounds to pursue success, walk out their God-designed purposes, and leave positive spiritual and moral legacies for their families.

Faith Life Now produces two television programs—*Fixing the Money Thing* and *Drenda*—as well as practical resources, conferences, and speaking events around the world.

Gary is also the president and founder of Forward Financial Group and the founding pastor of Faith Life Church, which has campuses in New Albany and Powell, Ohio.

Gary and Drenda, their five adult children and their spouses, and their grandchildren all reside in Central Ohio.

For additional resources by both Gary and Drenda, visit FaithLifeNow.com.

FORWARD
FINANCIAL GROUP

Would you like more information on how to get out of debt, safeguard your investments, and build wealth? Our associates at Forward Financial Group can show you how to get started!

Contact us at **ForwardFinancialGroup.com**.

FINANCIAL REVOLUTION
CONFERENCES

If you're a pastor or leader in your church, you probably have plenty of vision for your ministry. But do you have the money or resources you need to support the vision?

If your church is like most churches, the answer is probably *not quite* or even *no*.

Why?

We've found one of the biggest reasons is DEBT. So many Christians are being held *hostage* by debt.

Your people *WANT* to financially support the ministry and vision of your church, but many of them are living paycheck to paycheck with no hope of breaking free.

We can help.

For more than 25 years now, we've been working with churches of all sizes, helping them reach their goals and see their visions for their ministries become reality. And the best part is that this is completely free!

We help churches by helping their people. We can help *your church* by helping *your people*.

Learn more at **ftmtevent.com**.

Gary Keesee went from being completely desperate financially and physically to healthy and whole, paying cash for cars, building his home free from debt, starting multiple companies, and teaching hundreds of thousands of people about Kingdom living each week through television, ministry, and books just like this one.

What changed for Gary and how can it change YOUR LIFE?

Your answers are in the pages of THIS book series.

This isn't just another set of books with tips on how to fix your finances.

Full of fresh revelation, powerful examples from the Word of God, and inspiring personal stories about Gary and others who applied the foundational teachings from these five Kingdom principles in their own lives and experienced drastic change as a result, this series of books was written to help YOU experience real change in EVERY area of your life.

No matter your situation, there are answers. It's never too late.

You can have your own amazing story!

Join Gary Keesee on this incredible five-part journey of discovery that will completely revolutionize YOUR life… just like it did his.

This set contains paperback versions of Gary's complete *Your Financial Revolution* book series:

- *Your Financial Revolution: The Power of Allegiance*
- *Your Financial Revolution: The Power of Rest*
- *Your Financial Revolution: The Power of Strategy*
- *Your Financial Revolution: The Power of Provision*
- *Your Financial Revolution: The Power of Generosity*

Get your copy of the complete *Your Financial Revolution* five-book series at GaryKeesee.com.